AI

for Absolute Beginners

Learn AI the Easy Way — No Code, No Jargon.
Just Practical Tools You Can Use Right Now.

Written by
Eric LeBouthillier

AcraSolution | 2025 1st Edition
www.acrasolution.com

Preface

Who This Book Is For

This book is for everyday people curious about artificial intelligence — whether you're a student, small business owner, busy professional, or someone who simply wants to stay current with technology. If you've heard of tools like ChatGPT, Gemini, or AI art generators but aren't sure how to use them — this is your starting point.

You don't need any coding experience. You don't need a tech background. You just need the desire to understand how AI fits into real life — and how to use it to work smarter, save time, and explore ideas.

What You Can Expect

This is not a deep dive into machine learning theory or programming. Instead, this is a no-code, no-jargon guide designed to help absolute beginners:

- Understand what AI is (in plain English)
- Use beginner-friendly AI tools right away
- Apply AI to everyday tasks like writing, planning, organizing, and creating
- Avoid common beginner mistakes and myths
- Learn how to use AI responsibly and ethically

By the end, you'll have hands-on experience, a basic understanding of key AI tools, and the confidence to keep exploring.

AI is no longer the future — it's the present. This book will help you catch up, keep up, and move forward.

For permission requests or inquiries, contact the publisher through the website : www.acrasolution.com

LEGAL DISCLAIMER

This publication is intended solely for informational and educational purposes. It does not constitute legal, financial, medical, or professional advice. The content is not a substitute for consultation with qualified experts or licensed professionals in the relevant fields.

Portions of this work have been created or assisted by artificial intelligence (AI) tools. While every reasonable effort has been made to review, fact-check, and edit the content for clarity and accuracy, AI-generated information may occasionally contain errors, omissions, or generalized statements. The author and publisher do not guarantee the accuracy, completeness, or reliability of the information provided.

Readers are strongly encouraged to seek independent advice tailored to their personal circumstances from qualified legal, financial, healthcare, or compliance professionals before making decisions or taking action based on this content.

References to specific products, services, companies, websites, or technologies do not imply endorsement or affiliation unless explicitly stated. All trademarks and brand names mentioned remain the property of their respective owners.

The author and publisher disclaim any liability, loss, or risk incurred directly or indirectly from the use or misuse of this publication. This includes, but is not limited to, damages of any kind — including incidental, special, or consequential — arising out of the reliance on the material presented.

Table of Contents

CHAPTER 1

What Is AI (and Why Should You Care)?

AI in Plain English: No Jargon, No Math

Most small and mid-sized business leaders today are being asked to make decisions about AI — whether that's adopting new tools, safeguarding their operations, or even just evaluating a vendor's claims. But let's be honest: most of the AI talk out there sounds like it was written for PhDs or science fiction fans. That's a problem.

You don't need equations or computer science degrees to make smart, confident AI decisions. You need clarity, grounded insight, and a way to see through the noise. That's what this chapter is here to give you.

The Real Definition of AI — No Hype

At its core, artificial intelligence is the ability of a machine to perform tasks that typically require human intelligence. That's it. That includes things like recognizing speech, identifying objects in photos, summarizing text, predicting customer behavior, or answering questions.

AI is not a mind. It's not sentient. It's not "thinking" in any human sense. Most of today's AI systems are more like supercharged spreadsheets — very fast at detecting patterns, but totally dependent on the data and instructions we give them.

Where the Confusion Starts

The problem is that AI is a marketing buzzword now. Vendors, startups, and consultants all use the term "AI" to describe everything from basic automation to advanced machine learning. This leads to three common misconceptions:

- **AI is smarter than humans** — False. It's faster, not smarter.
- **AI understands context like a person** — False. It mimics understanding based on patterns in its data.
- **AI can replace human judgment** — Dangerous assumption. It can't assess ethics, nuance, or real-world consequences.

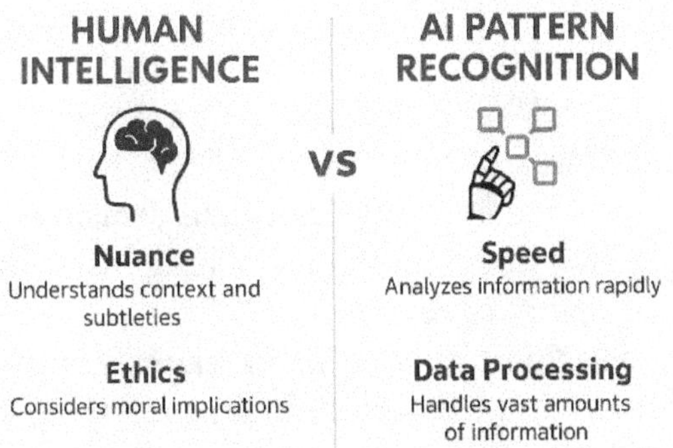

Think of AI as a Tool — Not a Colleague

The right mental model for AI is that of a very fast, very specialized intern. It can summarize 500 pages in 10 seconds, but it doesn't know what's important unless you tell it. It can generate reports, but it doesn't understand the business strategy behind them.

This means AI can be incredibly useful — if you know how to point it in the right direction, and if you don't assume it "knows" more than it really does.

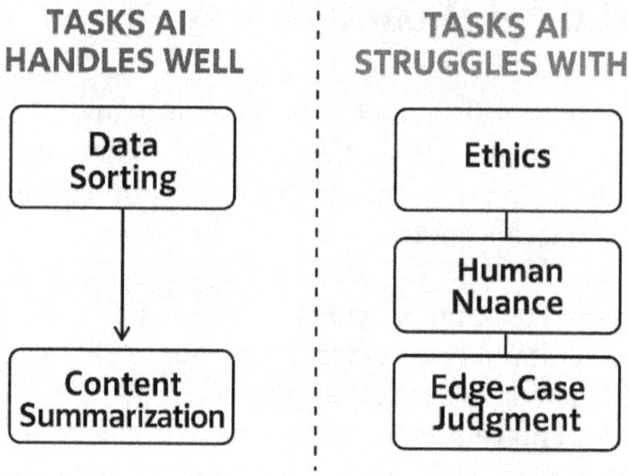

Tactical Best Practices

- Always ask: "What data is this AI trained on?" If you don't know, don't trust the output.
- Use AI for speed and scale, not final decisions.
- Keep a human in the loop for anything involving customers, money, or compliance.
- Treat AI as an amplifier — it'll make your processes faster, but not smarter unless you train it properly.

Common Pitfalls

- **Overtrusting the tool**: AI can make up facts ("hallucinate") if it doesn't know something.
- **Assuming it understands goals**: AI will optimize for what you *measure*, not what you *mean*.
- **Ignoring edge cases**: AI can fail catastrophically when things fall outside of its training data.

Real-World Example

What happened: A regional bank rolled out an AI-based chatbot to handle customer queries. It was trained on a dataset of past customer service transcripts, but no legal or compliance data.

What went wrong: The bot started giving financial advice it wasn't allowed to, including speculative answers about mortgage rates and investment products.

What we learn from it: AI only knows what it's trained on — and in regulated industries, that's a big risk. Any tool interacting with customers needs legal, compliance, and brand oversight from day one.

Checklist-Style Action Steps

- Define the task clearly before choosing any AI tool.
- Know your data: where it comes from, how recent it is, and what it covers.
- Build a process for human review before output is finalized.
- Limit AI's role in areas with legal, financial, or reputational risk.
- Document how and why AI is being used — this is key for trust and audits.

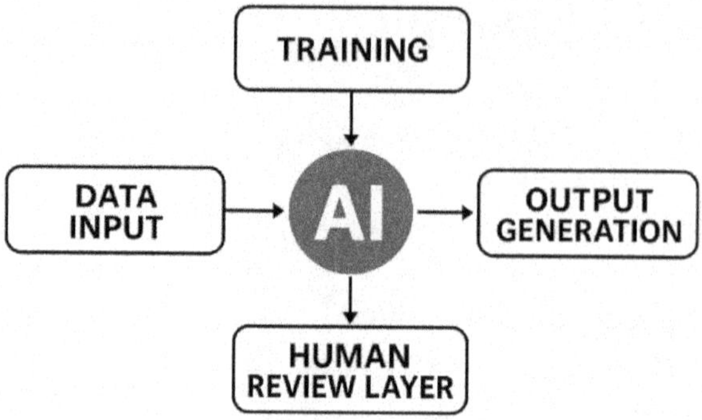

AI LIFECYCLE

Conclusion

AI doesn't need to be scary or mysterious. But it does need to be respected. When you strip away the hype, you're left with a very powerful tool — one that depends entirely on how well it's understood and managed.

Next Steps

In the next section, we'll look at exactly what today's AI tools can and can't do — with no hype and no assumptions. You'll walk away knowing which tasks you can delegate safely to AI, and which ones you never should.

What AI Can (and Can't) Do Today

If you're leading a business, you're likely being told that AI can do everything — from writing your marketing copy to making hiring decisions. That's not just misleading. It's dangerous. Knowing what AI can *really* do today — and what it absolutely can't — is the only way to use it wisely and safely.

Where AI Excels

AI is extremely effective in domains with clear data patterns and defined outcomes. It's not magic. It's math — well-trained and optimized to spot patterns faster than any human could.

AI STRENGTHS

STRENGTH	EXAMPLE TASK
Speed	Performing calculations
Pattern Recognition	Identifying trends
Data Processing	Analyzing large datasets
Summarization	Creating concise summaries

What AI Does Well:

- **Summarizing and categorizing**: It can condense reports, group customer inquiries, or tag files quickly.
- **Translating languages**: From English to Spanish to technical jargon.
- **Generating content drafts**: Emails, code snippets, marketing copy, or business memos.
- **Forecasting based on patterns**: Like churn prediction, product demand, or fraud detection.
- **Handling structured tasks at scale**: Sorting resumes, processing insurance claims, flagging anomalies.

In essence: AI shines when the rules are clear, the patterns are strong, and the risk is low.

Where AI Struggles

The flipside? AI is surprisingly brittle when asked to reason like a human. It doesn't understand nuance, ethics, or emotion. It guesses based on prior data, not lived understanding.

AI HANDLES	AI STRUGGLES
Data Summarization	Ethical Decisions
Language Translation	Human Emotions
Image Recognition	Context Understanding
Pattern Analysis	Common Sense

What AI Doesn't Do Well:

- **Making ethical decisions**: It can't weigh right from wrong, or interpret legal gray areas.
- **Handling edge cases**: If the situation hasn't been seen in training data, AI flails.
- **Reading between the lines**: Sarcasm, irony, and emotional tone are often misread or ignored.
- **Strategy and innovation**: AI can't imagine what hasn't already happened — it extrapolates, not invents.
- **Sensitive interpersonal contexts**: Like hiring decisions, HR issues, or crisis communications.

Real-World Example

What happened: A growing e-commerce platform used AI to auto-approve seller listings. It relied on image recognition and natural language processing to catch prohibited items and banned phrases.

What went wrong: The AI missed age-restricted products and deceptive health claims. The content was subtle — things like ambiguous wording or borderline imagery — and it hadn't been properly trained to detect these.

What we learn: AI is only as smart as the data you give it. And in high-stakes environments — regulatory compliance, legal liability, or brand trust — it's not enough to hope the system "gets it right."

Tactical Best Practices

- Use AI to support people, not replace them — especially in public-facing or regulated roles.
- Train AI systems on *your* data — generic models miss critical context.
- Design fallback procedures — what happens when AI fails?
- Audit AI output like you would an intern's work — fast doesn't mean accurate.
- Segment tasks by complexity — use AI for low-judgment, high-volume tasks first.

Common Pitfalls

- **Blind delegation**: Assuming the AI "understands" the task because it generates plausible results.
- **Overconfidence in scale**: The faster AI moves, the faster it can replicate a mistake — across thousands of outputs.
- **One-size-fits-all deployment**: Not every workflow benefits from AI. Many are better served by a simple script or human touch.
- **Failure to monitor**: AI performance degrades if you don't update its data and assumptions regularly.

Checklist-Style Action Steps

- ✅ Inventory your current tasks — sort them by risk and complexity.
- ✅ Identify 2–3 low-risk, high-volume areas where AI can help now.
- ✅ Establish human review steps for any public or customer-facing AI output.

- ✅ Document AI decisions, inputs, and changes — this helps with future audits.
- ✅ Set a quarterly AI performance review — what's working, what's not, what's next.

Conclusion

AI today is powerful, but narrow. It's a scalpel, not a Swiss Army knife. The sooner you treat it that way, the more value — and less risk — you'll get from your investment.

Next Steps

In the next section, we'll tackle a source of endless confusion: the difference between **AI, Machine Learning, and Automation**. These aren't interchangeable buzzwords — and understanding the difference could change how you buy software, hire talent, and structure your tech stack.

The Difference Between AI, Machine Learning, and Automation

Most people use these terms interchangeably. But in a business context, that's a mistake. Knowing whether a tool uses AI, machine learning, or basic automation isn't just academic — it affects how you evaluate risk, performance, and ROI.

What They Actually Mean

- **Artificial Intelligence (AI)**: Any system that mimics human intelligence to perform tasks. It includes logic, learning, perception, and problem-solving — but doesn't necessarily "learn" on its own.
- **Machine Learning (ML)**: A subset of AI. ML systems improve their performance over time by identifying patterns in data without being explicitly programmed to do so.
- **Automation**: Rule-based execution of tasks — without intelligence. Think scripts, macros, or bots that do what you tell them, exactly how you told them.

Everyday Business Examples

Function	Automation	Machine Learning	Artificial Intelligence
Invoicing	Auto-send PDFs to clients	Detect anomalies in invoice timing	Respond to payment questions via chatbot
Hiring	Schedule interviews	Screen resumes based on patterns	Conduct sentiment analysis in interviews

Marketing	Post on a schedule	Optimize ads based on click data	Generate campaign messaging dynamically

Why the Differences Matter

If a vendor claims their solution is "AI-powered," ask: is it actually learning and improving? Or is it just rule-based automation with a fancier UI?

If it's automation, great — you know exactly what you're getting. But if it's AI or ML, then it's also:

- Learning from your data
- Potentially changing over time
- Requiring testing, monitoring, and guardrails

This has massive implications for risk, compliance, and outcomes.

Real-World Example

What happened: A logistics firm adopted what they thought was an AI route optimization tool. In reality, it was basic automation — following fixed business rules that didn't adapt to changing traffic or weather.

What went wrong: Routes weren't updating dynamically. The system delivered the *same* route plans daily, even as conditions changed.

What we learn: Labeling something "AI" doesn't make it intelligent. If it can't learn from data and improve, it's automation — and needs manual updating.

Tactical Best Practices

- Always ask vendors to clarify: is this AI, ML, or automation?
- For AI/ML tools, request documentation on model training, accuracy, and performance monitoring.
- Match the tool to the problem: use automation for predictable tasks; AI/ML where patterns evolve.
- Require transparency: know what the system is doing and how decisions are made.

Common Pitfalls

- **Buying for the buzzword**: Teams choose "AI tools" that add complexity without real benefit.
- **Lack of monitoring**: ML systems drift over time — if you don't check performance, they degrade.
- **Confusing smart outputs with smart systems**: Just because the output looks sophisticated doesn't mean the system is.

Checklist-Style Action Steps

- ☑ Label each tool in your stack: automation, ML, or AI?
- ☑ Review AI/ML systems quarterly to ensure outcomes align with business goals.
- ☑ Train teams to recognize when a tool is acting predictably vs. adaptively.
- ☑ Write clear governance policies for AI/ML — who's responsible, what's tracked, how often it's reviewed.

Conclusion

These three terms — AI, ML, and automation — are not just buzzwords. They shape how technology behaves inside your business. Misunderstanding them leads to mismatched expectations, wasted spend, and increased risk. But used correctly, each offers unique value.

Next Steps

In the next section, we'll bring the conversation down to earth: **How AI Affects Your Job, Business, and Daily Life**. Whether you're a founder, manager, or employee, the ripple effects are already showing up. Let's make them work for you. that are often confused but critically different. Understanding what you're actually working with is the first step to making sure it serves your goals.. You'll walk away knowing which tasks you can delegate safely to AI, and which ones you never should.

How AI Affects Your Job, Business, and Daily Life

You don't have to be in tech to feel the impact of AI. It's already in your email inbox, your customer support workflows, and the software you use to manage teams. AI is becoming infrastructure — embedded across roles, industries, and decisions.

But what does that mean for you and your people?

For Employees: Augmentation, Not Elimination

Despite the headlines, most AI deployments today aren't replacing entire jobs. They're replacing tasks. For knowledge workers, this means AI acts more like a force multiplier:

- **Drafting emails, reports, or slide decks faster**
- **Generating code or formulas for repetitive problems**
- **Summarizing meetings or documents**
- **Handling routine support tickets**

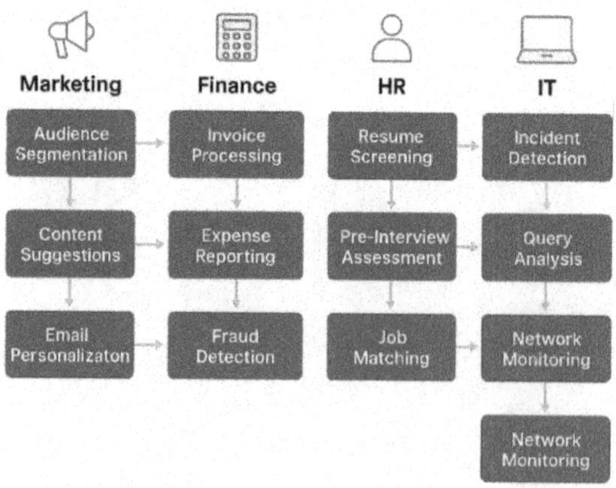

This shift requires upskilling — not because AI will take your job, but because knowing how to *use* it will become expected.

For Managers: Productivity Gains and New Risks

Managers are seeing AI tools promise 10x productivity — but with that comes responsibility. Leaders must decide:

- **Which tasks should stay human-controlled?**
- **How do we validate AI-generated outputs?**
- **Are we introducing risk (bias, hallucination, compliance issues)?**

The goal isn't to automate everything. It's to build hybrid workflows where AI handles the repeatable work, and humans apply judgment, creativity, and ethics.

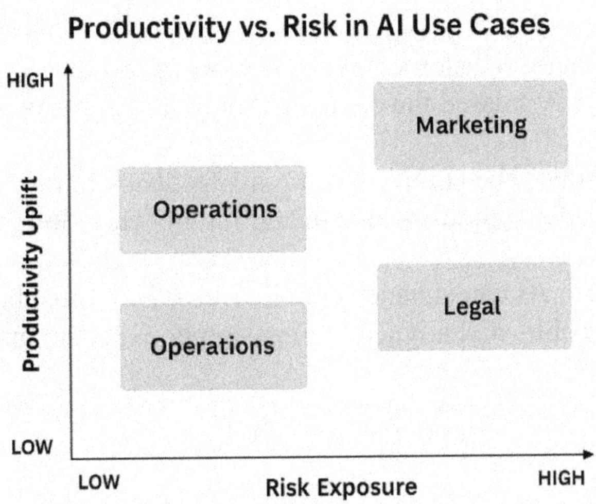

For Business Owners: Margin Expansion or Trust Erosion?

AI can shrink overhead fast. It can also backfire. Using AI to cut costs without controls may:

- **Confuse or alienate customers**
- **Expose the company to legal or PR risks**
- **Create a trust gap between leadership and teams**

But when applied transparently and strategically, AI can improve response times, customer service, and innovation velocity.

Real-World Example

What happened: A mid-sized SaaS firm rolled out AI to handle customer onboarding tutorials — using generative video and auto-written walkthroughs.

What went wrong: Customers felt the experience was impersonal and unclear. They missed the contextual help that humans provided.

What went right: The company used this feedback to retrain its AI tools, and added a "request a human" option in every flow.

What we learn: AI can enhance experiences — but must be optional, reversible, and aligned with customer expectations.

Tactical Best Practices

- Provide AI literacy training for all staff
- Build policies for when and how AI can be used in public-facing tasks
- Monitor productivity *and* sentiment when introducing AI tools
- Start pilot programs before scaling AI across departments
- Encourage human-AI collaboration instead of full replacement

Checklist-Style Action Steps

- ✅ Audit which AI tools are already in use across departments
- ✅ Define your company's stance: augmentation-first or automation-first?
- ✅ Create clear escalation paths for when AI outputs fail
- ✅ Engage employees in AI deployment decisions
- ✅ Track employee experience alongside business KPIs

Conclusion

AI is already in your business — even if you didn't approve it. Employees are experimenting. Vendors are embedding it in tools. Customers are noticing. You can lead this shift, or let it lead you.

Next Steps

Now that you've seen how AI shows up in real life, let's take a sharp turn: **Debunking the 7 Biggest AI Myths**. From sentient robots to "AI will steal your job," we'll separate fiction from fact — with real consequences for how you lead, invest, and compete.. Whether you're a founder, manager, or employee, the ripple effects are already showing up. Let's make them work for you. that are often confused but critically different. Understanding what you're actually working with is the first step to making sure it serves your goals.. You'll walk away knowing which tasks you can delegate safely to AI, and which ones you never should.

Debunking the 7 Biggest AI Myths

AI is one of the most misunderstood technologies in history. Every few years, it gets recast — either as our savior or our doom. In this section, we strip away the hype and misinformation, revealing what's real and what's not. The truth is powerful — especially when your business decisions depend on it.

Myth #1: AI Thinks Like a Human

The myth: AI has thoughts, beliefs, and self-awareness.

The reality: AI doesn't "think." It processes patterns in data to produce likely outcomes. There is no understanding, emotion, or intention. It's math — very fast, very advanced math.

Myth #2: AI Learns Like a Human

The myth: AI gets smarter with experience the same way we do.

The reality: AI "learns" only by identifying statistical patterns across massive datasets. It can't draw conclusions beyond those patterns or apply judgment to new, unseen contexts.

Myth #3: AI Is Always Objective

The myth: AI is neutral and free of bias.

The reality: AI reflects the data it's trained on — and if that data is biased, so is the system. Bias in training data leads to biased decisions in hiring, lending, marketing, and more.

Myth #4: AI Is Smarter Than People

The myth: AI will soon outthink humans in every area.

The reality: AI is faster than people at narrow tasks — not smarter across the board. It lacks common sense, context, and the ability to handle edge cases or moral reasoning.

Myth #5: AI Is Fully Autonomous

The myth: AI can operate without human oversight.

The reality: No responsible deployment of AI is fully hands-off. Even autonomous vehicles need human intervention at critical moments. AI must be supervised, audited, and governed.

Myth #6: AI Will Take All the Jobs

The myth: Mass unemployment is coming due to AI.

The reality: AI is transforming jobs, not eliminating them wholesale. It replaces tasks, not roles — and creates demand for new skills in prompt design, oversight, data validation, and integration.

Myth #7: AI Is Too Complex to Understand

The myth: Only data scientists and engineers can truly grasp how AI works.

The reality: You don't need to know the math to manage the risk. Understanding how AI behaves, what it's good at, and where it breaks is accessible — and essential — for every decision-maker.

Real-World Example

What happened: A retail brand paused AI expansion after public backlash against biased product recommendations. The AI had been trained on skewed historical data that reinforced stereotypes.

What went wrong: They failed to vet training inputs and didn't include a human review stage.

What we learn: Believing the "objectivity myth" blinded the team to risks. Bias in = bias out.

Tactical Best Practices

- Assume every AI system is fallible — build in checkpoints.
- Train teams to challenge outputs — not just accept them.
- Involve diverse stakeholders in training data selection.
- Build myth-busting into employee onboarding and vendor assessments.

Checklist-Style Action Steps

- ✅ Review your org's AI-related communications — are you overpromising?
- ✅ Educate staff on what AI is *not* — especially in risk-sensitive areas.
- ✅ Document where human oversight is required in all AI-powered tools.
- ✅ Run a "myth audit" on key AI tools: Is the team assuming too much?

Conclusion

The most dangerous thing about AI isn't what it can do. It's what people think it can do. Myths are comforting — or terrifying — but either way, they cloud your judgment. Seeing clearly is your competitive advantage.

Next Steps

You're now ready to engage with AI from a position of clarity, not confusion. In Chapter 2 — **The Tools You'll Use** — we'll move from theory to practicality: how to choose, evaluate, and integrate AI tools that align with your goals.. From sentient robots to "AI will steal your job," we'll separate fiction from fact — with real consequences for how you lead, invest, and compete.. Whether you're a founder, manager, or employee, the ripple effects are already showing up. Let's make them work for you. that are often confused but critically different. Understanding what you're actually working with is the first step to making sure it serves your goals.. You'll walk away knowing which tasks you can delegate safely to AI, and which ones you never should.

CHAPTER 2

The Tools You'll Use

ChatGPT (OpenAI) — Setup, Interface, Privacy Tips

For many business users, ChatGPT is their first hands-on experience with artificial intelligence. It's often presented as a magical assistant that can write anything, solve anything, and think like a pro. But to actually extract business value from ChatGPT, you need more than prompts — you need precision, policy, and a bit of restraint.

What ChatGPT Actually Is

ChatGPT is a conversational interface built on OpenAI's large language models — including GPT-3.5 and GPT-4. It doesn't "think" like a human. It predicts the most likely next words based on patterns in data. That makes it incredibly useful for tasks involving text — drafting, summarizing, converting, explaining — but also inherently limited.

It can't fact-check itself. It doesn't know what's true. And it only "remembers" what you give it in the chat, unless memory features are enabled.

Getting Set Up the Right Way

Start at chat.openai.com. You'll need an email address, phone verification, and optionally a payment method to access GPT-4 or plugins.

For businesses, it's critical to set up:

- **Separate company accounts** for each authorized user
- **Role-based access control** via OpenAI Teams or enterprise tiers
- **Clear usage policy** that outlines what kinds of data and use cases are allowed

Inside the Interface

Once logged in, the layout is minimal — but under the surface, there's important functionality:

- **Model Selector**: Toggle between GPT-3.5 (faster, cheaper) and GPT-4 (more advanced, accurate)
- **Memory Settings**: Decide whether the system retains user instructions across chats. Disabling this improves privacy.
- **Custom Instructions**: You can tell ChatGPT how to behave — what tone to use, how much detail to provide, or what it should always know about your business.
- **Chat History**: All past chats are logged unless explicitly disabled. Make sure this is managed if employees are using it for sensitive workflows.

What It's Good At — With Guardrails

ChatGPT is ideal for:

- Drafting initial versions of marketing copy, emails, proposals
- Brainstorming campaign ideas, interview questions, brand names
- Creating quick summaries of PDFs, meeting notes, or articles
- Converting technical jargon into plain language (or vice versa)
- Providing checklists or steps for SOPs, onboarding guides, training modules

But remember: ChatGPT doesn't verify data. If you ask it for citations, facts, or business metrics, always check the source.

Common Mistakes to Avoid

- **Pasting sensitive info**: Chat logs may be retained unless you've disabled memory and are on a privacy-compliant plan.
- **Using vague prompts**: The clearer the input, the better the output. "Write a report" yields fluff. "Write a 300-word summary of X for a CFO" gets results.
- **Relying on it blindly**: AI hallucinations are real — fake laws, misquoted data, or confident but incorrect logic.

Tactical Privacy & Compliance Tips

- Turn OFF memory unless you have legal clearance for persistent storage.
- Never input client names, payment data, contracts, or HR records.
- Use team access controls to manage visibility and audit logs.
- Document how you use ChatGPT — especially in client work or regulated industries.

Real-World Example

What happened: A marketing agency used ChatGPT to draft client blogs, assuming all outputs were factually sound. One post included fabricated quotes attributed to public figures.

What went wrong: The team didn't review outputs or validate information.

What we learn: ChatGPT generates "likely-sounding" content, not verified truth. Human review is non-negotiable.

Tactical Best Practices

- Create internal prompt templates for common workflows
- Assign a team lead to review outputs before publication or sharing
- Rotate monthly training sessions to refine prompt skills and review mistakes
- Build an FAQ for internal use to handle recurring privacy and output quality questions

Checklist-Style Setup Actions

- ✅ Register company-wide ChatGPT accounts with user roles
- ✅ Turn off memory unless explicitly required and approved
- ✅ Train users on prompt structure, hallucination risk, and output validation
- ✅ Establish data boundaries — what can/can't be entered into ChatGPT
- ✅ Designate reviewers for each major AI use case

ChatGPT can make your team faster — but only if it's used intentionally, reviewed carefully, and understood deeply.

Next Steps

Up next: **Claude AI, Gemini, and Perplexity — When to Use Each.** Not all tools are created equal, and each excels in different areas. Understanding their strengths and blind spots will help you choose the right one for every job.

Claude AI, Gemini, and Perplexity — When to Use Each

There's no one-size-fits-all AI tool. While ChatGPT dominates the conversation, other AI systems like Claude (by Anthropic), Gemini (from Google), and Perplexity (a retrieval-based assistant) are quickly gaining traction. Knowing how they differ — and when to use them — is critical for productivity, privacy, and performance.

Claude (Anthropic)

Claude is known for being more safety-conscious and better at following nuanced instructions — especially in longer documents.

Strengths:

- Exceptional at processing long text (over 100,000 tokens in Claude 3)
- Strong compliance posture and constitutional AI training (focus on ethical output)
- Often feels more "aligned" in tone for sensitive tasks (e.g., HR, legal summaries)

Best for:

- Summarizing long policies, contracts, and transcripts
- Writing with a more human tone in regulated industries
- Teams focused on security and conservative language generation

Gemini (Google)

Gemini integrates deeply with Google Workspace — Gmail, Docs, Sheets, and more. It's not just a chatbot — it's a layer across your entire productivity suite.

Strengths:

- Real-time integration with Google Docs, Sheets, Gmail, and Drive
- Live access to current data (via web-connected capabilities)
- Contextual awareness based on Workspace activity

Best for:

- Internal document drafting inside Google Suite
- Research using live internet data
- Fast turnarounds with access to up-to-date search results

Caution: Google's privacy policies mean business teams should be cautious about what data is exposed — always review account-level settings.

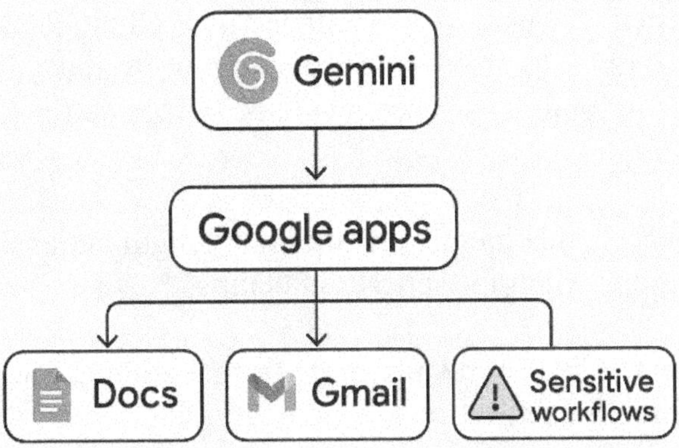

Perplexity

Perplexity is more of a research companion than a generalist writer. Its core differentiator is real-time information retrieval with citations.

Strengths:

- Accurate sourcing and footnotes (links to real documents)
- Fast and focused search-style answers
- Less prone to hallucinations in fact-based queries

Best for:

- Market research, competitor analysis, or fact-finding
- Validating claims or checking sources
- Generating short, accurate summaries with citations

Limitations: Not ideal for creative writing, long-form generation, or subjective prompts.

Real-World Scenario

What happened: A business consultancy used ChatGPT for legal summaries but ran into problems with token limits and hallucinations in long docs. They switched to Claude for legal-heavy content and Perplexity for research.

What worked: Claude handled nuance and length better. Perplexity provided citations when fact-checking claims.

What we learn: The best results come from matching tools to the task — not forcing one platform to do everything.

Tactical Best Practices

- Map AI tools to departments: marketing ≠ legal ≠ research
- Rotate tools in pilot programs and compare results
- Involve your data/privacy team before deploying any tool tied to external APIs
- Track output quality monthly and document performance gaps

Checklist-Style Action Steps

- ✅ Create internal guide: "Which tool to use when"
- ✅ Train teams on tool strengths/weaknesses
- ✅ Set permissions and privacy guardrails per platform
- ✅ Compare output from 2+ tools before high-stakes decisions

Next Steps

With general-purpose assistants mapped out, it's time to look at something more visual: **Canva Magic and Pictory — Design & Video with AI.** These tools aren't just for creatives — they're becoming essential to anyone building brand, training, or content assets fast.** Not all tools are created equal, and each excels in different areas. Understanding their strengths and blind spots will help you choose the right one for every job.

Canva Magic and Pictory — Design & Video with AI

You no longer need a design background or production budget to create brand-ready content. Tools like Canva Magic and Pictory have transformed the content creation landscape by giving everyday business users access to studio-grade assets at a fraction of the time and cost. Whether you're launching a new product, scaling a marketing campaign, or documenting internal training, these tools offer massive time savings — and empower teams to focus more on message than medium.

Why Visual and Video AI Matters

Visual content drives modern business. Slide decks, video explainers, social media clips, product demos — they're essential for engagement, conversion, and education. But they're also resource-intensive.

AI changes that. It offloads the first 80% of the creative grunt work, leaving your team to refine and direct instead of start from scratch. This shift unlocks speed and scale, especially for small teams without full-time designers or video editors.

Canva Magic: Fast, Flexible Design Without the Designer

What It Is

Canva is already a household name for intuitive drag-and-drop design. Canva Magic refers to its suite of AI features that supercharge productivity by generating text, visuals, and layouts with minimal input.

Key AI Features

- **Magic Write**: An AI copy generator for emails, headlines, ad scripts, and more.
- **Magic Design**: Turn a prompt (or even a rough idea) into a full-fledged slide deck or branded layout.
- **Text to Image**: Describe an idea — "a secure cloud workspace for SMBs" — and generate custom imagery to match.
- **Magic Edit & Magic Erase**: Remove or alter parts of a design image directly inside the platform.

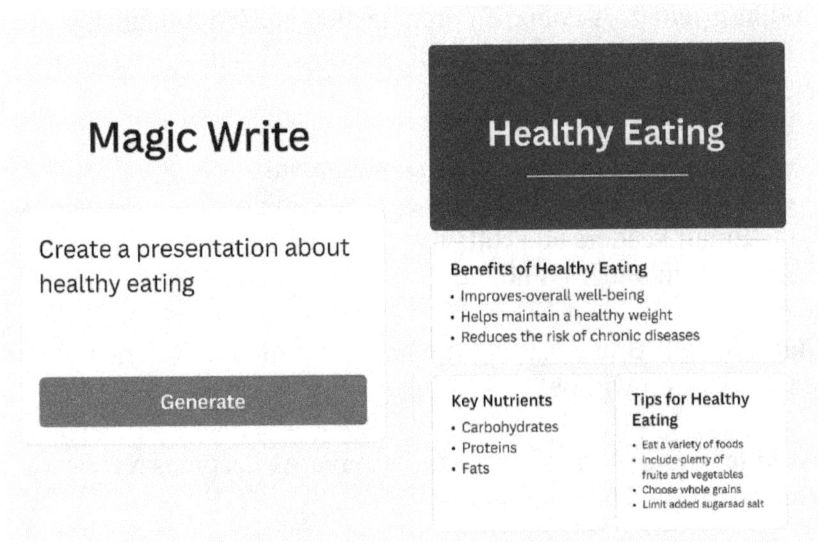

Strategic Use Cases

- **Marketing**: Auto-generate social media series, ad layouts, and email banners.
- **Sales Enablement**: Create decks, one-pagers, or proposal templates in minutes.
- **HR and Internal Comms**: Design onboarding guides, culture decks, policy explainers.

What to Watch For

- **Visual Overload**: More output means more clutter. Train your team to prioritize clarity over aesthetics.
- **Template Dependency**: AI-generated designs can feel repetitive. Use them as drafts, not final products.
- **Brand Consistency**: Without controls, teams may create off-brand materials. Load brand kits and lock core templates.

Real-World Example

What happened: A nonprofit organization needed to launch a fundraising campaign across email, social, and web. Using Canva Magic, one marketer created:

- A full slide deck for internal alignment
- Branded LinkedIn and Instagram graphics
- Email headers and calls-to-action
  —all in under 48 hours.

What worked: Brand assets were already loaded into Canva. AI sped up creation without sacrificing quality.

Lesson learned: With proper setup, Canva AI becomes a creative partner — not just a tool.

Pictory: From Blog to Broadcast in Minutes

What It Is

Pictory is an AI video tool that turns long-form written or video content into short, engaging videos. It's ideal for repurposing blogs, podcasts, webinars, and scripts into professional-looking assets — with voiceovers, music, and visuals.

Key AI Features

- **Script-to-video**: Input a blog post or draft, and get a narrated, captioned video in minutes.
- **Video Summarizer**: Upload a webinar or Zoom call, and Pictory extracts highlights and creates short-form video content.
- **Auto-captioning**: Ensures accessibility and improves engagement on silent autoplay platforms.

Strategic Use Cases

- **Content Marketing**: Convert blogs into YouTube Shorts or LinkedIn posts.
- **Training & L&D**: Turn SOPs and onboarding docs into visual microlearning.
- **Customer Success**: Produce FAQ explainers or feature walkthroughs.

What to Watch For

- **Stock Footage Dependence**: Too much canned imagery can hurt authenticity. Customize when stakes are high.
- **Voice Quality**: Auto-generated narration is improving, but human-recorded options still outperform in tone.
- **Editing Limitations**: Pictory is fast, but not precise. Keep Adobe or Final Cut in the loop for high-profile pieces.

Real-World Example

What happened: A SaaS company turned every blog into a short LinkedIn video using Pictory. They:

- Generated a year's worth of video content from existing blogs
- Increased engagement by 240% compared to static image posts
- Freed up the content team to focus on strategy and partnerships

Lesson learned: Repurposing > reinvention. AI video is about reach, not perfection.

Tactical Best Practices

- Build an approval workflow for all AI-generated content
- Store final assets in organized libraries tagged by use case and audience
- A/B test AI vs. human-generated assets for performance
- Standardize a feedback loop — let your team flag issues with tone, clarity, or branding

Checklist-Style Action Steps

- ✅ Set up your Canva brand kit and lock core templates
- ✅ Create a weekly AI content calendar using both tools
- ✅ Establish a "first-draft" AI rule: human review required for anything external
- ✅ Pilot Pictory with blog-to-video tests across three personas

Zapier AI — Automating Work Without Coding

AI-generated content is only as useful as the workflows that deliver it. That's where automation comes in — and Zapier AI is a game-changer for teams that want to eliminate manual steps without writing code.

Zapier has long connected apps like Gmail, Slack, Google Sheets, and Trello. But its new AI layer goes a step further: it helps you describe your automation needs in plain English — and builds them for you. You don't need a developer. You just need a process.

What Makes Zapier AI Different

Traditional automation platforms rely on step-by-step rule building. Zapier AI changes that by allowing:

- **Natural language workflow creation**
- **GPT-powered content enrichment within Zaps**
- **Smart branching logic** based on conditions, data scores, or AI outputs

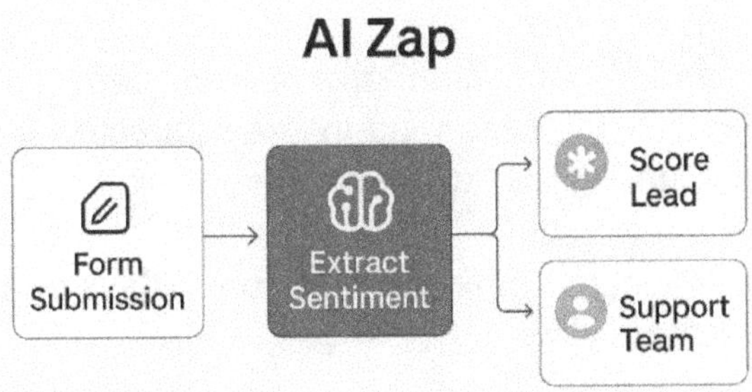

Strategic Use Cases

- **Sales Ops**: Automatically qualify leads, enrich contact data, and assign to reps.
- **Recruiting**: Parse resumes, analyze sentiment in cover letters, and tag by role fit.
- **Support**: Route tickets based on urgency, customer tier, or sentiment detected via AI.
- **Admin**: Generate task summaries from form inputs, notify approvers, and update dashboards.

What to Watch For

- **Garbage In, Garbage Out**: Poor form design or input structure ruins output quality.
- **Blind Trust in AI Steps**: Always review outputs when summarizing or scoring with GPT.
- **Hidden Costs**: Every Zap and AI call can consume task limits quickly — budget accordingly.

Real-World Example

What happened: A 15-person SaaS firm used Zapier AI to automate lead intake:

- Clients filled a form on the website
- Zapier used GPT to summarize project scope
- If budget > $10K, lead went to Sales Director; else, it triggered automated nurture emails

What worked: Response time dropped from 2 days to 2 hours. Lead conversion increased 34%.

Lesson learned: Automation isn't about volume — it's about velocity and relevance.

Tactical Best Practices

- Start by mapping every repeated task or handoff in your daily operations
- Train one team member per function (Sales, Ops, HR) as a Zap owner
- Keep AI steps isolated and reviewable — especially for text generation or summarization
- Use naming conventions, folders, and tags for Zap hygiene and scalability

Checklist-Style Action Steps

- ✅ List 10 most repeated manual processes by team
- ✅ Use Zapier AI builder to prototype 3 workflows in plain English
- ✅ Test each workflow for 2 weeks, measuring time saved and errors avoided
- ✅ Create a documentation template to onboard future Zap builders

Conclusion

Together, Canva Magic, Pictory, and Zapier AI create a full-stack creative and execution pipeline. You can design, publish, and automate without bottlenecks or backlogs — if you use them intentionally, review their outputs, and continuously improve based on feedback.

These aren't just tools. They're levers for scale, quality, and responsiveness in your business — and every SMB team should be taking advantage.

Bonus: 5 Free AI Extensions That Instantly Save Time

You don't need a full platform subscription to benefit from AI. Many of the most impactful AI-powered time savers are free browser extensions — lightweight tools that slip into your daily workflows and quietly remove friction. These aren't flashy experiments or productivity theater. These are serious time-savers for real business users.

Below are five proven, trusted extensions that integrate into everyday tools like Gmail, Google Docs, Chrome, LinkedIn, and your calendar. Each one comes with specific use cases, real-world caveats, and configuration tips so your team can get instant ROI.

1. Compose AI — Write Emails and Docs at Lightning Speed

What It Does

Compose AI is a Chrome extension that brings GPT-powered autocompletion, rephrasing, and drafting directly into your browser. It works across Gmail, Google Docs, LinkedIn, and most text inputs.

Strategic Use Cases

- Write or summarize emails faster with auto-suggest and inline generation
- Rephrase messages based on tone (e.g., make it more persuasive or concise)
- Auto-complete standard replies and reports

Key Tips

- Use the // command to insert AI drafts instantly
- Customize tone and formality settings in the toolbar
- Works best when combined with templates and your own snippets

What to Watch For

- Doesn't integrate well with Outlook
- Can misfire on longform documents — best for short/medium tasks

2. Tactiq — Real-Time Meeting Transcripts + AI Highlights

What It Does

Tactiq transcribes meetings in real-time (Zoom, Google Meet, MS Teams), then uses AI to summarize action items, decisions, and next steps. The free tier gives you basic transcript + summary features — enough to transform how you capture meetings.

Strategic Use Cases

- Sales calls: auto-capture client pain points and next actions
- Internal syncs: turn messy team meetings into actionable summaries
- Interviews: tag keywords and sentiment across sessions

Key Tips

- Integrates with Google Drive and Notion
- Use highlight and emoji reactions to train the AI what matters
- Combine with Otter.ai or Fireflies.ai for multi-system redundancy

What to Watch For

- Privacy warnings in regulated environments — always notify participants
- Summary quality improves with consistent formatting and moderation

3. Monica – Your Right-Click AI Assistant for Research

What It Does

Monica adds a right-click AI menu to your browser. Highlight any text and choose "Explain," "Summarize," "Translate," or "Rewrite." Think of it as ChatGPT, but embedded in every webpage.

Strategic Use Cases

- Summarize long articles or policy PDFs on the fly
- Translate internal documents quickly across global teams
- Rewrite confusing text into plain English instantly

Key Tips

- Customize voice and tone settings in Monica dashboard
- Use the sidebar for multi-step research and citations

What to Watch For

- Limited customization unless you upgrade to Pro
- Sometimes stalls on large or non-selectable text blocks

4. Merlin – Turn Any Website Into a Prompt Engine

What It Does

Merlin overlays an AI sidebar on any webpage — letting you ask questions, summarize, draft emails, or brainstorm ideas directly from your browser. It connects with OpenAI's API and offers robust integrations.

Strategic Use Cases

- Research: Ask context-aware questions about long pages or reports
- Email: Auto-generate replies or summarize threads
- Drafting: Pull ideas from pages into marketing copy or decks

Key Tips

- Great for solo founders or analysts reading deep content
- Pin the toolbar for quick access to smart features

What to Watch For

- Requires OpenAI account for some GPT-4 features
- Free tier includes limited requests per day

5. Gmail Smart Prompts by Flowrite (Beta) — AI-Boosted Email Autopilot

What It Does

While Gmail already includes Smart Compose, Flowrite's Chrome extension layers in more power. You get full-message generation, tone shifting, and task-based automation — like following up, rescheduling, or replying to intro emails.

Strategic Use Cases

- Inbox zero: Rapidly triage and respond to non-urgent emails
- Executive assistants: Draft updates and approvals faster
- HR and recruiting: Respond to applicants and interview scheduling

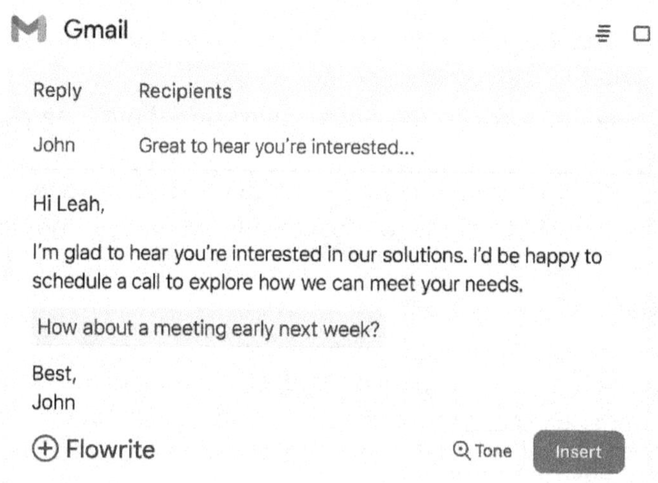

Key Tips

- Connects with your Gmail calendar and CRM
- Prompts improve over time as it learns from your responses

What to Watch For

- Email privacy: Never use with confidential communications
- Draft quality varies — always review before sending

Real-World Use Scenario

What happened: A five-person consulting team installed all five tools and assigned each to a different department lead:

- BizDev used Compose AI to streamline proposals
- Ops used Tactiq to automate client meeting notes
- Legal used Monica to decode regulatory documents
- Research used Merlin for competitive analysis
- Admin used Flowrite to manage email backlogs

Result: Across five weeks, time-to-output dropped 40%. AI tools filled the gaps that formal systems didn't cover.

What we learn: These small extensions compound into major workflow gains — without vendor contracts, training, or platform shifts.

Tactical Best Practices

- Create a team-wide AI extension policy: what's allowed, where, and how
- Use a shared dashboard to log wins and friction from each extension
- Train each team on one tool at a time — don't overwhelm with five at once
- Appoint an "AI Extension Steward" to manage privacy settings and updates

Checklist-Style Action Steps

- ☑ Pick 2 extensions that solve your team's biggest friction points
- ☑ Train users with real-world scenarios, not product demos
- ☑ Track time saved and workflow improvements across 2 weeks
- ☑ Review all browser extension privacy settings quarterly

Conclusion

You don't need an AI department to benefit from artificial intelligence. These five free extensions prove that small upgrades — strategically deployed — can yield immediate time and clarity benefits for your business. Each tool becomes a micro-skill for your team. Added together, they change the pace of how you work.

Next Steps

Coming up in Chapter 3: **Prompting Like a Pro (Without Being One)**. You'll learn how to write clear, powerful AI instructions that generate useful output the first time — with zero jargon or technical guesswork.

CHAPTER 3

Prompting Like a Pro (Without Being One)

The Beginner's Prompt Formula (Role + Goal + Context)

Prompting isn't a technical skill — it's a thinking skill. And the difference between a vague prompt that produces fluff and a clear one that delivers business-ready output isn't magic. It's structure.

That's where the **Role + Goal + Context** formula comes in. This chapter breaks it down, shows it in action, and gives you practical guidance to use it across every major task in your business.

Why Prompts Matter More Than You Think

Every AI output is only as good as the input you give it. Garbage in, garbage out — except in this case, vague in, vague out.

Your prompt is the blueprint. It tells the AI:

- Who it should act like (Role)
- What you want it to do (Goal)
- What information it should consider (Context)

Without that structure, AI tools will either guess — often incorrectly — or return a generic response that wastes your time.

What Happens Without a Clear Prompt

Let's say you type:

"Help me write a marketing plan."

That could mean a 1-page strategy. Or a 20-page PDF. Or just some tips.

Now compare it to:

"Act as a senior SaaS marketing strategist. Write a 1-page marketing plan to help us launch a new time-tracking tool for remote teams. Focus on positioning, channels, and metrics."

Same request. But the second one gives the AI:

- A clear persona to emulate (Role)
- A specific outcome to generate (Goal)
- Enough business details to tailor the advice (Context)

The difference in quality — and usefulness — is night and day.

Step-by-Step Breakdown: Role + Goal + Context

1. Role: Tell the AI Who to Be

AI doesn't know your audience. But it can mimic tone, expertise, and style — *if* you assign it a role.

Example roles:

- A cybersecurity compliance officer
- A B2B sales enablement manager
- A technical recruiter for mid-sized firms

Why this works: It narrows the AI's voice and decision style. Instead of generic advice, you get output shaped by domain logic.

Real prompt add-on:

"Act as a CFO advising a startup on budgeting for cloud services."

2. Goal: Tell the AI What to Deliver

Avoid verbs like "help," "suggest," or "tell me about." Use specific, production-oriented verbs:

- "Write a…"
- "Draft a…"
- "Summarize…"
- "Create a checklist…"

The clearer the action, the better the output.

Compare:

- ❌ "Help me with onboarding"
- ✅ "Draft a 5-step onboarding guide for remote engineers joining a fintech company"

3. Context: Add the Right Background

This is where most prompts fall apart. If you don't tell the AI what matters — audience, use case, tone, platform — it'll guess. And it'll guess wrong.

What to include:

- Who the audience is
- What format or length you need
- What tone or style you want
- What data or constraints the AI should follow

Example:

"Create a LinkedIn post in a professional but conversational tone. Audience: early-stage SaaS founders. The goal is to share 3 insights from our recent report on churn reduction. Keep it under 300 words."

Prompt Formula in Action: Business Scenarios

Marketing

"Act as a direct response copywriter. Draft a 5-email nurture sequence for leads who downloaded our ebook on business automation. Audience: SMB owners. Goal: convert to demo bookings. Tone: clear, no fluff."

HR

"You're an HR policy consultant. Create a short internal FAQ on using ChatGPT at work. Audience: 100+ person remote-first team. Emphasize privacy and tone expectations. Keep it under 400 words."

Finance

"As a startup CFO, build a 3-part checklist to evaluate the cost impact of using generative AI tools across departments. Audience: founders and ops leaders."

Common Prompting Pitfalls to Avoid

❌ Too Short

"Write a blog post about sales" — No role, no tone, no context. Result: bland content.

❌ Vague Goals

"Help me summarize this" — Summarize into what? For whom? How detailed?

❌ No Audience Target

AI can't infer who you're writing for. "Create a presentation" looks different for investors vs. interns vs. regulators.

Advanced Variations on the Formula

As you grow comfortable, you can start layering:

- **Constraints**: "Limit to 300 words. Include 3 action verbs."
- **Voice borrowing**: "Mimic the style of Jason Fried."
- **Comparative prompts**: "Write this as both a conservative and an aggressive strategy."
- **Multi-format prompts**: "Create a version for email and one for a Notion page."

These give you control without needing technical know-how.

Real-World Example

What happened: An operations lead at a 50-person tech firm needed to draft a handbook section on AI use at work. Their first prompt:

"What should employees know about AI?"

They got vague, general tips.

Revised prompt:

"Act as an HR consultant. Write a 500-word internal policy on using generative AI tools like ChatGPT in the workplace. Audience: non-technical staff. Include tone guidance, privacy restrictions, and acceptable use cases."

Result: The second output was usable with minor edits — saving hours.

What we learn: Prompt clarity is a skill multiplier.

Tactical Best Practices

- Use a template with Role, Goal, and Context fields
- Always specify audience and tone, even for internal drafts
- Keep prompts under 3 sentences when possible — clarity over cleverness
- Use numbers: word count, list items, or structure targets help AI format well
- Save your best prompts in a team wiki or SOP

Checklist-Style Action Steps

- ✅ Build a prompt template for your top 5 business workflows
- ✅ Create "prompt kits" by team (marketing, sales, HR, etc.)
- ✅ Review prompts quarterly — refine based on real output quality
- ✅ Assign someone on each team to be the prompt coach or quality reviewer
- ✅ Train new hires to start with Role + Goal + Context by default

Conclusion

Prompting is not about getting the AI to understand you. It's about instructing the system with the same clarity you'd expect from your best employee. With Role + Goal + Context, any team member — regardless of technical skill — can start producing high-quality outputs.

You're not "talking to AI." You're briefing a powerful assistant. How well it delivers depends entirely on how well you structure the task.

Next Steps

In the next section, we'll take this further: **Smart Prompting with Follow-Ups and Edits**. You'll learn how to refine, reframe, and repurpose outputs like a professional — even if your first draft flops.

Smart Prompting with Follow-Ups and Edits

Most people stop after their first prompt. That's the single biggest mistake in working with AI.

The real power of prompting isn't in the first request — it's in the follow-ups, the refinements, and the ability to steer the conversation. Great prompting is less like typing a Google search and more like managing a junior team member who can improve rapidly when given feedback.

In this chapter, we'll show you how to use follow-ups, clarifications, and structured edits to shape AI output that's truly useful. Whether you're drafting copy, developing training docs, creating business strategy, or analyzing data, the ability to iterate and refine will save you hours.

Why You Should Never Stop at One Prompt

Every first prompt is a draft.

Even a well-structured Role + Goal + Context prompt may not hit the mark the first time. That doesn't mean the AI is broken — it means you're still shaping the outcome.

Like a designer creating logo variations or a writer working through headlines, the best AI users treat prompts as a creative brief that evolves. Each response gives you information to build on.

The Core Moves: Follow-Up, Refine, Redirect

1. Follow-Up for Depth or Clarity

The AI gives you an outline. Now what?

"Expand bullet #3 into a detailed paragraph."

"Can you rewrite that with simpler language for non-technical readers?"

These are clarifying commands. You're not asking for a new result — you're asking it to go deeper.

2. Refine the Output with Style or Structure Guidance

Got the right substance, but the wrong tone?

"Rewrite this in the tone of a COO explaining a change to employees."

"Make this more concise — keep it under 200 words."

These are editing prompts. Use them to polish, not start over.

3. Redirect with New Instructions

Maybe the original wasn't even close. Don't start over — redirect.

"Instead of a customer email, turn this into an internal Slack announcement."

"Assume we're presenting this to skeptical investors — revise to focus on ROI."

Redirecting helps you salvage structure or insight while changing course.

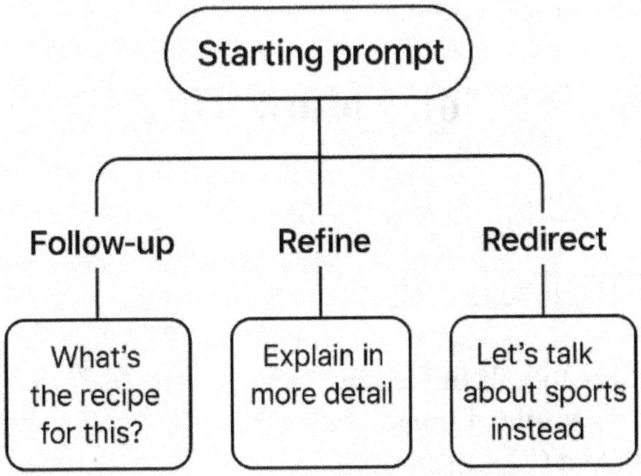

Prompt Iteration in Real Scenarios

Scenario: Creating a Policy Memo

1. **Prompt 1**: "Act as a workplace compliance officer. Draft a 300-word memo about the use of AI tools like ChatGPT in customer communications."
2. **Follow-Up**: "Add a note on the risk of data leakage."
3. **Refine**: "Make it sound more human — less legalese."
4. **Redirect**: "Turn this into a two-slide summary deck instead of a memo."

Each step builds on the last — no need to start from scratch.

Scenario: Writing Job Descriptions

1. "Write a job description for a product marketing lead at a B2B SaaS startup."
2. "Make it more concise — less than 500 words."
3. "Add a bullet for AI tooling familiarity."
4. "Rewrite the tone to sound more founder-led and scrappy."

This kind of iterative prompting lets you get to final draft quality in 10 minutes instead of 3 hours.

Best Practices for Follow-Ups

Use Specific Edits

Don't say "make it better." Say:

- "Cut this to half the length."
- "Add examples for each bullet."
- "Include a CTA at the end."

Ask for Alternatives

- "Give me three variations."
- "What's a bolder version of this message?"
- "Rewrite this as if I'm targeting enterprise clients."

Layer Prompts Intentionally

Think like an editor:

1. First draft for structure
2. Second pass for tone
3. Final pass for polish, CTA, or formatting

Real-World Use Case: Reworking a Sales Script

What happened: A B2B founder used AI to write an outbound call script. The first prompt was:

"Create a phone script to pitch our SaaS platform to small businesses."

Problems: It sounded robotic, was too long, and didn't include the pricing question.

Follow-Up Path:

- "Make this more conversational and under 2 minutes."
- "Add a response for 'We don't have budget right now.'"
- "Create two versions: one for cold leads, one for warm referrals."

Result: By version 4, the founder had a polished, segmented script usable by junior SDRs.

Lesson: Prompting isn't about perfect wording — it's about coaching the tool to your real need.

Editing Techniques that Work with AI

1. Inline Edits

Copy and paste part of the AI's output into a new prompt:

"Rewrite this paragraph to focus on benefits, not features."

2. Comments to Self

Use brackets or notes:

"Revise this [make it more urgent, cut jargon]."

3. Highlight and Replace

"Keep the structure but replace the examples with finance use cases."

Prompt Flow Templates

For Business Writing

1. Prompt: “Draft a one-pager explaining our new benefits program.”
2. Follow-Up: “Make it more conversational — employees, not execs.”
3. Edit: “Add a FAQ section.”
4. Redirect: “Can you turn this into a short welcome video script instead?”

For Technical SOPs

1. “Act as a DevOps lead. Document how to onboard a new engineer into our GitHub workflow.”
2. “Add screenshots placeholders.”
3. “Now turn this into a training checklist.”

For Client Communication

1. “Write a project update email for a client 2 weeks behind schedule.”
2. “Make it more empathetic but still firm.”
3. “Add a line offering a revised timeline.”

Tactical Best Practices

- Treat the AI like a first-draft assistant, not a final editor
- Use clear, actionable verbs in every follow-up
- Save successful prompt sequences to re-use later
- Review final drafts yourself — AI saves time, not judgment
- Use bullet format for tight control of output formatting

Checklist-Style Action Steps

- ✅ Create prompt flow templates by role (sales, ops, HR)
- ✅ Build a feedback phrase library: tone, length, audience, urgency
- ✅ Encourage "three-step prompts" on your team: draft → revise → repurpose
- ✅ Run side-by-side tests of first-prompt vs. refined-prompt outputs
- ✅ Establish prompt review as part of onboarding for new hires

Conclusion

Prompting isn't about knowing what to ask once. It's about knowing how to work with AI like an assistant who improves with your direction. By mastering follow-ups and smart edits, you unlock quality and precision — without rewriting from scratch or settling for generic output.

The real power of AI prompting is iterative. And your next version is always one edit away from excellent.

Next Steps

In the next section, we'll break down advanced "Act As" frameworks — roles and mental models that consistently produce higher-quality output with fewer instructions. Get ready to take prompting beyond basics and into pro-level territory.

“Act As” Frameworks to Supercharge Results

There’s one prompt trick that consistently generates better results — across industries, departments, and skill levels. It’s simple, powerful, and completely underused:

“Act as...”

This isn’t just semantics. Telling an AI who to “be” — not just what to do — unlocks sharper logic, clearer tone, and more business-relevant outputs. In this chapter, we’ll break down the psychology, strategy, and real-world application of “Act As” prompts, giving you a full toolkit to guide AI into behaving like a specialist, not a generalist.

Why the “Act As” Model Works So Well

Large language models aren’t truly intelligent. They don’t reason or understand — they predict. But what they predict is shaped by the patterns of language associated with certain personas.

When you say:

“Act as a startup CTO writing a postmortem after a data breach.”

...the model draws on language patterns from thousands of technical postmortems, CTO blogs, and cybersecurity playbooks. That alignment gives you:

- **More accurate voice**
- **Higher signal-to-noise ratio**
- **Less generic advice**

Core "Act As" Categories That Drive Results

1. Profession-Based Roles

These are the most direct — align AI output to a job function.

- Act as a product manager at a growth-stage SaaS firm
- Act as a compliance auditor writing a board memo
- Act as a hiring manager at a fintech startup

These roles guide tone, precision, and structure based on profession norms.

2. Audience Emulators

Flip the frame: act as your reader or stakeholder.

- Act as a skeptical CFO reviewing this proposal
- Act as a junior employee reading an onboarding email
- Act as a prospective customer comparing vendor quotes

Why this matters: It shifts the AI's frame of reference — from outputting *information* to crafting *relevance.*

3. Scenario-Specific Experts

Use roles that fit the moment — not the org chart.

- Act as a legal expert preparing for a contract negotiation
- Act as a workshop facilitator planning a remote team offsite
- Act as a customer support agent handling a product recall

These prompts excel at task-based outputs like scripts, agendas, policies, and checklists.

4. Style-Based Creators

Need a tone shift? Style roles solve for that.

- Act as a TED speaker explaining this concept to a non-technical audience
- Act as a UX copywriter writing microcopy for a signup page
- Act as a coach giving blunt but encouraging feedback

Real-World "Act As" Prompt Examples

Marketing

"Act as a content strategist at a cybersecurity startup. Write a blog post introducing our zero-trust webinar to mid-sized business IT managers. Tone: confident, educational, not salesy."

Legal

"Act as a privacy compliance officer. Summarize this draft policy in plain English for non-legal stakeholders. Keep it under 400 words."

HR

"Act as a culture and people leader. Create a 3-slide summary of our Q3 engagement survey for exec review."

Sales

"Act as a B2B sales engineer. Craft a follow-up email after a discovery call, tailored to a COO concerned about integration friction."

Customer Success

"Act as a support team lead. Write a knowledge base article on troubleshooting billing errors, aimed at small business users."

Elevate "Act As" With Supporting Instructions

The "Act As" command is the role — but the best results come when you also layer:

- **Tone** ("Make it confident and upbeat")
- **Audience** ("Writing for technical leadership")
- **Output format** ("Turn this into a table and 3 bullets")
- **Constraints** ("Keep it under 2 minutes read time")

Example Full Prompt:

"Act as a hiring manager at a fast-growing startup. Create a 4-paragraph rejection email that's empathetic but clear. Audience: mid-career candidates who made it to final rounds. Tone: respectful, firm. Keep under 250 words."

This produces thoughtful, on-brand, usable content.

Common Mistakes With “Act As” Prompts

✖ Too Vague:

“Act as a business expert.”

Fix:

“Act as a B2B SaaS growth strategist targeting mid-market logistics companies.”

✖ No Supporting Detail:

“Act as a marketer.”

Fix:

“Act as a product marketer launching a new AI-driven hiring tool. Target: HR tech buyers. Goal: explain use cases, not features.”

✖ Mismatch Between Role and Task:

“Act as a lawyer” … then ask for informal marketing copy.

Fix:

Choose a role whose voice aligns with your desired output — or explicitly combine roles.

Combining "Act As" Roles With Prompting Workflows

Strategy Prompt Flow

1. Act as a strategy consultant
2. Draft a 1-pager on competitive positioning
3. Follow-up: "Add market share estimates and key trends"
4. Refine: "Now summarize it for exec review in 3 bullets"

Internal Comms Prompt Flow

1. Act as an internal comms director
2. Write a Slack update for a delayed product launch
3. Follow-up: "Add a link to internal roadmap"
4. Redirect: "Turn this into a short Loom script for the CEO to narrate"

Tactical Best Practices

- Start with real roles from your team or industry
- Add audience and use-case details in the same prompt
- Save successful "Act As" prompts by department
- Use prompt chaining: change the "Act As" role mid-session to shift perspective (e.g., legal → marketing → customer success)

Checklist-Style Action Steps

- ✅ Build a shared "Act As" prompt bank for your organization
- ✅ Train teams to select role + tone + task before writing any prompt
- ✅ Audit your current AI usage — replace generic prompts with role-based versions
- ✅ Add "Act As" guidance into internal prompt templates and SOPs
- ✅ Test response differences across 3-4 roles for the same prompt to choose best output

Conclusion

"Act As" isn't just prompt decoration — it's a strategy. It gives AI a lens, a voice, and a sense of priorities. When used thoughtfully, it transforms outputs from generic to high-context, usable, and aligned.

Whether you're drafting a deck, scripting a message, or planning a product launch, the right role unlocks the right reasoning. And unlike real people, AI will never say "That's not my job."

Next Steps

In the next section, we'll open the vault: **Copy-Paste Prompt Library for Everyday Tasks**. You'll get high-performing, real-world prompts — tested and templated — for sales, hiring, content, ops, and more.

Copy-Paste Prompt Library for Everyday Tasks

The fastest way to get value from AI tools isn't learning theory — it's having proven prompts that just work. This section gives you a ready-to-use library of high-performing, copy-paste prompts for real business tasks.

Each one follows the Role + Goal + Context model and is designed to be easily customized for your industry or team. These are field-tested, executive-ready, and optimized for immediate ROI.

📩 Email + Communication

Prompt: Executive Summary Email

"Act as a chief of staff. Write a 3-paragraph email summarizing today's leadership meeting. Audience: department heads. Include key decisions, action items, and deadlines. Tone: direct and informative."

Prompt: Sales Follow-Up

"Act as an account executive. Write a concise follow-up email to a lead after a demo. Emphasize product fit, next steps, and a call to book the implementation call. Keep it under 150 words."

Prompt: Internal Announcement

"Act as an HR communications lead. Draft a Slack message announcing the new PTO tracking system. Tone: friendly and clear. Include link to the internal doc and a contact for questions."

📋 Operations + Processes

Prompt: SOP Drafting

"Act as an operations manager. Write a step-by-step SOP for onboarding new vendors, including compliance, contracts, and payment setup. Output as bullet points. Audience: finance and ops teams."

Prompt: Meeting Agenda

"Act as an executive assistant. Create a 5-point agenda for a 30-minute check-in between the CEO and marketing head. Focus: Q3 planning, hiring status, KPIs."

Prompt: Risk Mitigation Plan

"Act as a risk officer. Draft a 1-page outline for mitigating AI misuse in content generation across marketing and customer success teams."

🧠 Strategy + Planning

Prompt: SWOT Summary

"Act as a strategy consultant. Create a SWOT analysis for a mid-sized cybersecurity firm expanding into healthcare. Output as a table with 3 bullet points per quadrant."

Prompt: Competitive Analysis Brief

"Act as a product marketer. Write a 500-word competitive summary comparing our AI analytics tool against two major competitors. Highlight price, features, and integrations."

Prompt: Roadmap Summary

"Act as a product manager. Summarize the next 90-day roadmap for internal stakeholders in plain English. Highlight features, dependencies, and user impact."

📣 Marketing + Content

Prompt: LinkedIn Post

"Act as a founder. Write a LinkedIn post sharing lessons from our first failed product launch. Keep it authentic, short (under 300 words), and end with a question to the reader."

Prompt: Newsletter Intro

"Act as a B2B content strategist. Draft a short, engaging intro paragraph for this month's product newsletter. Theme: AI adoption in SMBs. Audience: operations and IT leads."

Prompt: Social Media Campaign Ideas

"Act as a brand strategist. Generate 5 social media campaign concepts to promote our new AI video tool to creators. Format: campaign name, concept, platform suggestion."

🧑💼 Hiring + HR

Prompt: Job Description

"Act as a hiring manager. Write a concise job description for a remote customer support lead with AI experience. Include top 3 responsibilities and 3 required skills."

Prompt: Interview Questions

"Act as a recruiter. Create 5 behavioral interview questions for a growth marketer position. Focus on testing adaptability and campaign ownership."

Prompt: Onboarding Email

"Act as an HR coordinator. Draft a welcome email for a new engineering hire starting next Monday. Include start time, who to meet, and a Slack invite link."

🧾 Finance + Admin

Prompt: Budget Justification Summary

"Act as a finance lead. Summarize the Q2 AI tools budget for exec review. Include line items, usage trends, and cost-per-seat analysis. Tone: concise and numeric-focused."

Prompt: Reimbursement Policy Memo

"Act as a controller. Write a 300-word memo updating the team on new travel reimbursement limits. Include effective date, examples, and contact for questions."

Prompt: Procurement Email

"Act as a procurement officer. Write a vendor request email asking for a new pricing breakdown and SLA confirmation. Audience: SaaS account manager."

📊 Data + Analysis

Prompt: Survey Summary

"Act as a data analyst. Summarize key findings from our employee engagement survey. Include top 3 trends, two quotes, and one next action. Audience: exec team."

Prompt: KPI Report Draft

"Act as a performance analyst. Draft a 1-page KPI report for customer onboarding. Metrics: time to activation, NPS, and support tickets. Format: table + bullet insights."

Prompt: Dashboard Instructions

"Act as a BI lead. Write step-by-step instructions for filtering the sales pipeline dashboard in Looker. Audience: sales reps unfamiliar with Looker."

Tactical Best Practices

- **Customize** the role and task slightly to fit your company's language
- **Save** your favorites into a team wiki or Notion prompt bank
- **Test** prompts monthly against your top tools (ChatGPT, Claude, etc.)
- **Refine** with follow-ups after each paste — this is a starting point, not the finish

Checklist: How to Use This Prompt Library

- ✅ Copy any prompt that matches your current need
- ✅ Edit the role or audience slightly if needed
- ✅ Paste into your AI tool of choice (ChatGPT, Claude, Gemini, etc.)
- ✅ Follow up: ask for a shorter version, add examples, or adjust tone
- ✅ Save final prompts in your team's SOP or internal playbook

Conclusion

You don't need to memorize how to write prompts. You need a fast-start kit. This library gives you a working foundation — across departments — to get immediate traction with AI.

These prompts can be used as-is or customized over time. Each one replaces an hour-long blank page session with a 5-minute jump-start.

Next Steps

In the next section, we'll show you how to build your own **Prompt Bank using Notion or Google Sheets** — so your team has a single source of truth for AI effectiveness across your workflows.

Building Your Own Prompt Bank with Notion or Sheets

You don't need a massive AI strategy to start seeing serious time savings. Sometimes, the most powerful shift you can make is creating a simple, central place to store and reuse the prompts that already work.

That's what a **Prompt Bank** is — a shared, searchable home for your best AI instructions. Whether you're using ChatGPT, Claude, Gemini, or Perplexity, a prompt bank removes guesswork, improves quality, and speeds up adoption across your team.

This section will walk you through building your own using tools you already know: **Notion** or **Google Sheets**.

Why a Prompt Bank Is a Force Multiplier

Most teams treat prompting like improvisation. That works until it doesn't.

Without a system, you get:

- Repeated trial and error
- Inconsistent tone or quality
- Delayed results when key people are unavailable

But with a shared prompt bank:

- Teams get up to speed faster
- High-performing prompts get reused (and improved)
- You build institutional memory for your AI strategy

Step 1: Choose Your Tool — Notion vs Sheets

🗃 Notion

Ideal for teams already using it for docs, wikis, and projects. Offers:

- Tagging and filtering
- Embedded examples
- Rich formatting (dropdowns, buttons, links)

📊 Google Sheets

Better for simple tabular structure, fast filtering, and export. Works well if you want:

- Lightweight interface
- Excel-like views
- Easy CSV backup or sync with other tools

Tip: Use Notion if you want rich formatting, and Sheets if you want speed and simplicity.

Step 2: Create the Right Columns or Properties

No matter the tool, your prompt bank needs structure. Here's a minimum viable setup:

Field	Description
Prompt Title	Short, clear label (e.g., "Sales Demo Follow-Up")
Full Prompt	The full copy-paste text, using Role + Goal + Context

Field	Description
Use Case	What it's for (e.g., sales, hiring, content)
Output Format	Email, slide, policy, checklist, etc.
Audience	Who the output is meant for
Tool	ChatGPT, Claude, Gemini, etc.
Owner/Creator	Optional — who created or vetted it
Notes	Helpful tweaks, versioning, or links

Bonus fields:

- Tags (Notion) or Labels (Sheets)
- Effectiveness rating
- Last updated

Step 3: Seed It with Your 10 Most-Used Prompts

You don't need to start big. Start with:

- 2–3 prompts per department
- Tasks you repeat weekly
- Your best outputs so far

Examples:

- "Act as a recruiter. Write a 3-paragraph rejection email."
- "Act as a support manager. Create a 5-step guide for refund processing."
- "Act as a founder. Draft a 60-second LinkedIn video script."

Use the Role + Goal + Context model for each. Store them cleanly — one row/card per prompt.

Pro tip: Include at least one tested follow-up command with each (e.g., "Now make it shorter and punchier.")

Step 4: Organize for Fast Retrieval

Prompt banks don't work if they're buried.

In Notion:

- Add a main Prompt Bank page to your company wiki
- Use database view with filters by function or audience
- Create a simple "Request a Prompt" button using forms

In Sheets:

- Use filters at the top row
- Color-code by department or use case
- Freeze the header row for visibility

Step 5: Train Your Team to Use It

A prompt bank only works if people use it. Make this part of team workflows:

- **Add to onboarding**: New hires get a link and short training
- **Weekly use-it sessions**: 15 mins to test or contribute a prompt
- **Prompt of the Week**: Highlight one every Monday with examples

Create a simple intake form:

- Name
- Prompt purpose
- What you tried
- What you want it to do better

This turns your prompt bank into a living, improving system.

Step 6: Track What Works (and What Doesn't)

Not every prompt is gold. Tag them:

- ● Use Often
- ○ Needs Tuning
- ● Don't Use

Ask:

- Did it save time?
- Was the output usable with minimal editing?
- Did others on the team reuse it successfully?

In Notion, use a thumbs-up property or comment thread. In Sheets, use color or a 1–5 rating.

"If it saved someone 20 minutes, it probably belongs in your bank."

Bonus: Use AI to Document Your Prompts

You can even use AI to document your best AI use.

"Summarize this ChatGPT thread into a reusable prompt and instructions."

Then store that.

"Turn this into a formatted Notion entry: title, use case, prompt, and 3 notes."

That's how you go from chaotic chat history… to an operational asset.

Real-World Example: SMB Team Wins Back 6 Hours/Week

What happened: A 20-person services firm had four people using ChatGPT inconsistently. One ops manager built a shared prompt bank in Notion over a weekend.

What went right:

- Created 25 prompts across sales, support, HR, and content
- Linked from the company's internal wiki
- Held a 30-min session to show how to use + contribute

Result: Within a month, prompt use doubled, and the team estimated saving 6 hours/week — not by writing more, but by writing *once, well, and reusing.*

What we learn: AI scale doesn't require more prompts — just better systems.

Tactical Best Practices

- ✅ Always test prompts before saving
- ✅ Include one good follow-up prompt per entry
- ✅ Use filters: by team, tone, format, and tool
- ✅ Review and update prompts monthly
- ✅ Link examples or outputs in Notion comments
- ✅ Create a submission form for others to contribute

Checklist: Building Your Prompt Bank

- Choose Notion or Sheets as your foundation
- Set up fields: Title, Prompt, Use Case, Format, Audience, Notes
- Seed it with your 10 highest-value prompts
- Add at least one tested follow-up per prompt
- Link it in onboarding and SOPs
- Train your team: how to search, submit, and refine
- Revisit monthly to prune, promote, or retire

Conclusion

Prompting is a skill. A prompt bank is a strategy.

If you want AI adoption to scale beyond the early adopters in your org, you need a simple, structured, and visible place for your best work to live. Notion and Sheets make it possible in an hour. The gains compound every week.

Your time is too valuable to write the same instructions twice. Build the bank. Save the future.

Next Steps

Coming up next: **Chapter 4: AI in Your Daily Life** — where we shift from the workplace into the real world, showing how the same prompting principles can help with personal productivity, learning, parenting, travel, and more.

Chapter 4

AI in Your Daily Life

Automating Email Replies, Planning, and Calendar Tasks

The average knowledge worker spends over two hours a day on email, meeting planning, and calendar juggling. That's not strategic work — it's overhead. AI can now handle much of that friction without extra software or steep learning curves. You just need to know how to use it.

This section shows how to automate and accelerate your communication and scheduling tasks using tools already built into Gmail, Outlook, and your calendar. You'll learn what AI can do well here — and how to avoid common mistakes that waste time instead of saving it.

Smart Email Replies

Whether you're in Gmail or Outlook, AI-enhanced replies are now embedded in the interface — or just a browser extension away.

Use Case: Responding to Customer Inquiries

Prompt:

"Act as a customer support rep. Write a professional response to this email, confirming receipt, setting expectations for follow-up within 24 hours, and using a helpful tone."

Paste the original email content after the prompt. The AI will structure a clean, tone-aligned reply.

Use Case: Following Up on Sales or Proposals

Prompt:

"Act as a sales coordinator. Write a follow-up email referencing the proposal sent last Thursday. Include a quick summary, restate the value, and suggest a 15-minute call this week."

Tip: Save time by creating a prompt template bank directly in your inbox tool using snippets or tools like TextExpander.

Calendar Coordination Without the Back-and-Forth

One of AI's most useful roles is being your scheduling assistant. Tools like Gmail Smart Compose, Microsoft Copilot, or add-ons like x.ai help eliminate the "What time works for you?" loop.

Use Case: Scheduling a Meeting

Prompt:

"Suggest three time slots based on my availability next week and write an email to a client proposing them. Tone: professional but warm."

You can integrate this with your calendar access to make it even smarter. Tools like Clockwise or Reclaim.ai also apply AI to auto-schedule deep work vs. meeting time.

Use Case: Declining or Rescheduling Politely

Prompt:

"Act as an executive assistant. Write a brief, polite email declining a meeting invite due to a conflict. Suggest two alternative time slots and express interest in meeting soon."

Daily Planning Made Automatic

You can now use AI inside tools like Google Calendar or Microsoft 365 to:

- Summarize your day
- Flag conflicts
- Suggest focus blocks

Use Case: End-of-Day Summary for Tomorrow

Prompt:

"Act as a productivity coach. Review my schedule for tomorrow and summarize it in bullet points. Note key meetings, prep time needed, and open blocks for deep work."

Use Case: Creating a Priority List

Prompt:

"Based on tomorrow's calendar, create a priority list of the top 3 things to prepare for. Include short action steps for each."

Tools like Motion or Sunsama layer AI directly onto your calendar for task reshuffling, meeting prep, and end-of-day wrap-ups.

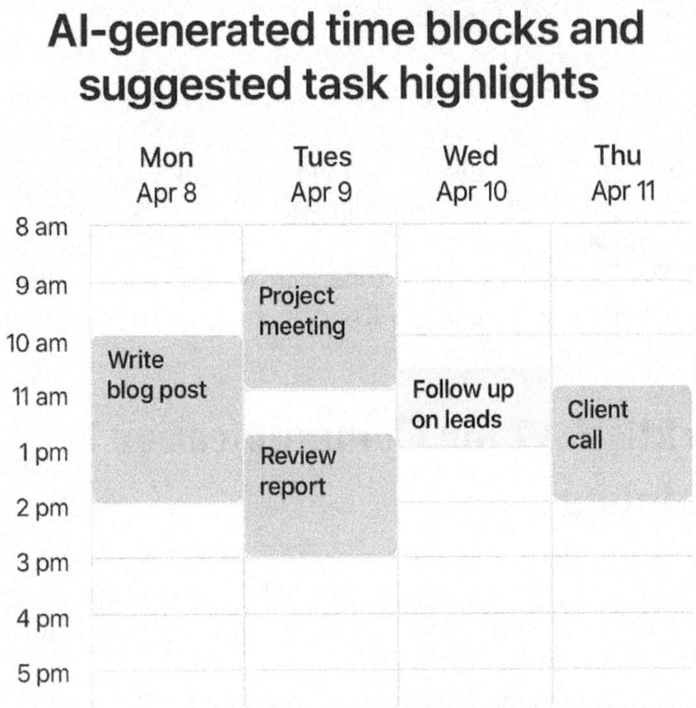

Common Pitfalls to Avoid

Even helpful AI can become a bottleneck if used poorly. Watch out for:

- **Over-polishing**: Emails can sound robotic if too scripted. Always scan for human tone.
- **Misunderstanding urgency**: AI doesn't always know when a response is time-sensitive unless you tell it.
- **Blind trust**: Always review calendar slots and meeting times — AI can miss overlapping events.

"Use AI as your assistant — not your final approver."

Tactical Best Practices

- Use role-based prompts: Tell the AI who it's pretending to be.
- Save go-to prompts for meetings, declines, or quick replies.
- Connect AI to your calendar when safe — review permissions first.
- Check AI responses for tone, clarity, and time accuracy.
- Use browser extensions like Superhuman AI, GrammarlyGO, or Outlook Copilot.

Checklist: AI for Communication & Scheduling

- Respond to emails with templated AI prompts
- Create auto-scheduling responses with suggested slots
- Use daily or weekly planning summaries
- Review generated content for tone and timing
- Store prompts in a snippet tool or prompt bank

Real-World Example: Solopreneur Saves 10+ Hours/Month

What happened: A freelance designer began using AI prompts for all scheduling and proposal follow-ups. She created a prompt folder and used shortcuts via Gmail and Calendly.

What went right:

- Created standard client follow-up and reminder messages
- Used AI to draft calendar availability emails
- Reduced back-and-forth by 70%

What we learn: Even solo operators can scale their professionalism and response time with lightweight AI.

Conclusion

Email and scheduling aren't just admin tasks — they're how work gets coordinated. Done well, they speed everything else up. Done poorly, they introduce delay, miscommunication, and burnout.

The right prompts and a few AI helpers can reclaim hours from your day — without changing how you work, just how you start.

Next Steps

In the next section, we shift from communication to content — specifically, **how AI can boost your writing productivity inside tools you already use: Google Docs and Microsoft Word.**

Writing Smarter with AI in Google Docs & Word

Word processing hasn't changed much in decades — until now. With AI tools built directly into Google Docs and Microsoft Word, writing can shift from a solitary grind to a collaborative, context-aware workflow. Whether you're drafting a report, revising a proposal, or brainstorming ideas, AI can act as your co-writer, proofreader, and productivity assistant.

This section shows you how to get practical results by integrating AI into your everyday documents — and how to avoid the noise that can derail your writing.

What AI Can Do Inside Docs and Word

Built-in AI tools like Google Duet AI and Microsoft Copilot offer functionality directly within your word processor. These tools can:

- Generate content from prompts
- Rewrite, shorten, or improve tone
- Summarize long documents
- Suggest outlines or formats
- Create action items from notes

Use Case: Drafting a Project Proposal

Prompt:

"Write a 2-page project proposal for redesigning our client onboarding process. Include an overview, objectives, timeline, and success metrics. Tone: confident and consultative."

Place your cursor in a blank doc and paste this prompt. Tools like Google Docs with Duet AI will generate a structured first draft within seconds.

Optional Follow-Up Prompt:

"Now rewrite the objectives section to be more client-focused and action-oriented."

Use Case: Refining Existing Writing

Let's say you've written an internal memo, but it feels too long or wordy.

Prompt:

"Rewrite this paragraph to be more concise and direct, while keeping a professional tone."

Paste the paragraph right after the prompt. Both Docs and Word AI tools will deliver cleaner, easier-to-read versions — without losing meaning.

You can also use AI to:

- Convert passive voice to active
- Split long paragraphs
- Add subheadings

Use Case: Brainstorming in Document Format

AI can help you generate ideas before you start outlining.

Prompt:

"Give me five different approaches for launching a new employee wellness program, including pros and cons for each."

Follow up with:

"Turn option 2 into a one-page briefing note."

Using AI for Revision, Not Just Drafting

AI is even more powerful in the editing phase:

- Highlight a sentence or paragraph and ask for alternatives
- Ask it to rephrase in plain English
- Use tone adjustment tools to make writing warmer or more assertive

Tip: Customize the tone

- "Make this friendlier"
- "Add a sense of urgency"
- "Make this feel like it's coming from the CEO"

These micro-tweaks save time, reduce back-and-forth, and improve clarity.

Common Pitfalls to Avoid

- **Over-relying on AI tone**: Machine-generated tone can be flat. Always read it aloud.
- **Forgetting the audience**: AI doesn't always know who you're writing for — be explicit in prompts.
- **Skipping editing**: AI output isn't final copy. Use it as a fast first draft, not a finished product.

"AI helps you write faster. You still have to write smart."

Tactical Best Practices

- Use the comment feature to prompt AI within context (e.g., "Make this more persuasive")
- Label prompt types in your doc margin: Draft, Rewrite, Summarize, Expand
- Save common prompts in a sticky note or header area of the document
- Test different phrasings — small changes in prompt wording can dramatically shift output quality
- Set tone, audience, and intent up front — every time

Checklist: Smarter Writing in Docs & Word

- Draft first paragraphs using AI co-author tools
- Use inline suggestions for clarity and flow
- Rephrase for tone or audience as needed
- Insert summary bullets at the end of long sections
- Save prompts for reuse at the top or in comments

Real-World Example: HR Manager Speeds Policy Writing

What happened: An HR manager responsible for employee policy documents began using Google Docs with Duet AI to streamline updates and drafts.

What went right:

- Used prompts like "Write a plain-language summary of this 3-page policy"
- Drafted new onboarding materials in half the time
- Edited tone of legal notices to be more employee-friendly

Result: Cut document prep time by over 50% and improved clarity across the board.

What we learn: Editing and tone refinement can be just as valuable as generating new content.

Bonus: Smart Templates for Repeat Work

Build out templates for common business writing, then pair them with prompt shortcuts:

- Proposal template + "Fill this with onboarding redesign plan"
- Press release shell + "Announce product update in friendly, factual tone"
- Slide outline + "Add speaker notes for each bullet"

Save these in a shared folder and label each with best-use scenarios.

"Templates + prompts = repeatable writing speed."

Conclusion

You don’t have to be a better writer to get better writing — you just need to pair your process with smart AI prompts. Whether you're working in Word or Docs, the key is clarity: in your structure, your tone, and your expectations from the tools.

With even a handful of tested prompts and a little practice, you’ll write faster, clearer, and more confidently — without sacrificing quality.

Next Steps

Coming next: **Personal Budgeting with AI-Powered Templates** — where we look at how smart spreadsheets, auto-categorization, and financial prompts can make managing money less painful and more proactive.

Personal Budgeting with AI-Powered Templates

Budgeting used to mean spreadsheets full of formulas and hours of manual data entry. Today, AI simplifies everything from monthly planning to expense tracking — even predicting where you might overspend.

This section walks you through how to use AI inside Google Sheets, Excel, and budgeting platforms to take control of your finances with less effort and more confidence. It's not about complex math — it's about smarter workflows.

AI-Ready Budgeting Templates That Save Time

Modern spreadsheet tools come with AI features baked in — or they can be enhanced with free extensions and integrations.

Start with a solid base:

- Monthly Budget Tracker
- Expense Categorizer
- Cash Flow Forecaster
- Subscription Audit Sheet

Tip: Choose the tool you already use

- Google Sheets: Ideal for real-time sharing and simple AI add-ons like GPT for Sheets.
- Excel (365): Powerful with Microsoft Copilot and advanced forecasting.

Use Case: Creating a Personalized Monthly Budget

Prompt:

"Act as a financial advisor. Create a monthly budget based on a $4,500 monthly income. Include fixed expenses (rent, insurance), variable (groceries, gas), and savings goals. Format for Google Sheets."

Tools like ChatGPT or Copilot can generate a clean table with categories, amounts, and formulas.

Follow-up prompt:

"Add conditional formatting to highlight overspending in red."

Use Case: Categorizing Past Transactions Automatically

Upload or paste your bank transactions into a Google Sheet. Then use a formula-enhanced prompt:

Prompt:

"Classify these expenses by category: food, housing, utilities, subscriptions, shopping, and savings. Output in Column B."

With GPT for Sheets or a similar extension, this auto-tags every row.

Advanced prompt:

"Flag any subscription over $20 and suggest if it looks unused based on frequency."

Use Case: Forecasting Future Expenses

AI can also help plan ahead — especially for variable spending like holidays, travel, or quarterly bills.

Prompt:

"Based on the last 3 months of spending data, forecast the next month's expenses by category. Highlight areas that may go over budget."

This helps surface patterns — and stops surprises before they happen.

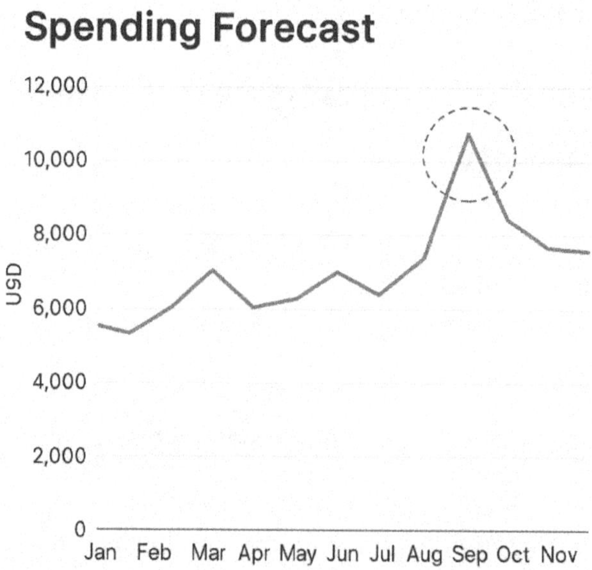

Using AI with Popular Budgeting Platforms

You don't need to live inside spreadsheets. Many people use apps like:

- YNAB (You Need A Budget)
- Monarch Money
- Tiller

These tools often allow data export, which you can enhance with AI. For example:

Prompt:

"Summarize this CSV export into a spending report. Highlight 3 key trends and 2 recommendations."

This turns raw data into decision-ready insight.

Common Pitfalls to Avoid

- **Ignoring privacy**: Don't upload sensitive financial info into unsecured AI platforms. Use local or encrypted tools.
- **Assuming AI is always accurate**: Always double-check formulas and totals — especially in Excel.
- **Automating too soon**: Start manually to understand your flow, then add AI to simplify — not replace — your thinking.

"AI should make your money clearer, not more mysterious."

Tactical Best Practices

- Always test AI-generated sheets before trusting them
- Use conditional formatting for red/yellow/green budget zones
- Add note columns: "AI says I overspend here. Why?"
- Schedule a weekly 10-minute review — with AI summary prompts
- Export app data monthly for deeper analysis

Checklist: Smarter Budgeting With AI

- Choose your tool: Sheets, Excel, or budgeting app
- Start with a base budget or use AI to generate one
- Auto-categorize expenses using prompt-based formulas
- Apply conditional formatting for budget alerts
- Forecast next month using trend prompts
- Review and refine weekly — not once a year

Real-World Example: Family of Four Cuts $400/month in Hidden Spend

What happened: A two-parent household used Google Sheets and ChatGPT to overhaul their budget.

What they did:

- Exported bank statements
- Used AI to classify expenses
- Flagged 7 unused subscriptions
- Forecasted future school-related expenses

Result: Recovered $400/month and created a sustainable, trackable plan — no accountant needed.

What we learn: Simplicity, transparency, and AI-powered categorization can lead to real savings fast.

Bonus: Automate Alerts and Summaries

Using extensions or formulas, you can:

- Email yourself a weekly summary: "Top 3 spending areas + red flags"
- Trigger notifications when categories go over budget
- Create visual dashboards for partners or accountability

Prompt:

"Build a dashboard in Google Sheets showing monthly savings, expense trends, and alerts. Include charts."

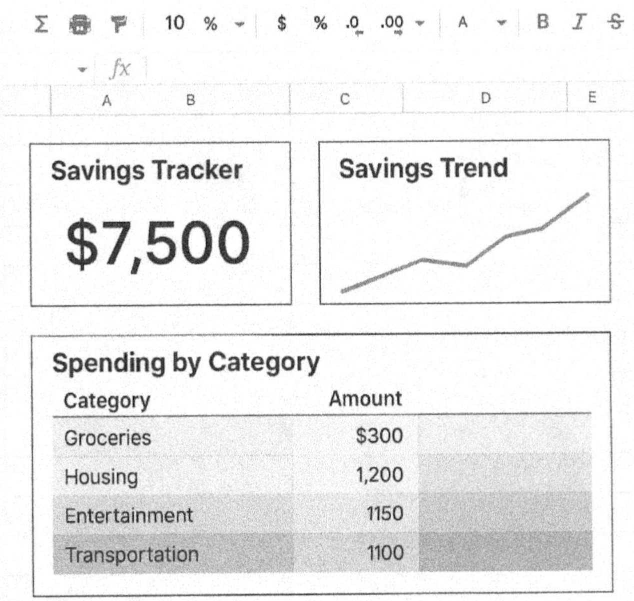

Conclusion

Budgeting doesn't need to be overwhelming. With AI, you can create clarity, consistency, and even creativity in how you manage money.

The key is to use prompts and templates that match your real life — and make small adjustments weekly. You'll gain financial confidence without spreadsheets taking over your weekend.

Next Steps

Up next: **AI Meal Planning, Travel Itineraries, and Reminders** — where we apply similar planning logic to simplify your home life and personal routines with the help of AI.

AI Meal Planning, Travel Itineraries, and Reminders

What if your daily routines — meals, trips, and tasks — didn't require so much mental load? AI now helps simplify the logistics of everyday life. With just a few smart prompts, you can build a healthy meal plan, map out a vacation, or automate reminders that keep life running smoothly.

This section covers how to use AI to save time and mental energy on personal logistics — whether you're organizing a grocery list or planning a cross-country trip.

AI for Meal Planning

Meal planning isn't just about recipes — it's about reducing decision fatigue, saving money, and minimizing food waste. AI can now:

- Recommend meals based on dietary goals
- Auto-generate shopping lists
- Create prep schedules

Use Case: Weekly Meal Plan by Diet Type

Prompt:

"Act as a nutritionist. Create a 5-day meal plan for a vegetarian family of four. Include breakfast, lunch, dinner, and snacks. Keep prep under 30 minutes per meal."

Follow-up prompt:

"Now generate a consolidated shopping list for all ingredients by grocery category."

Use Case: Budget-Friendly Planning

Prompt:

"Create a low-cost weekly meal plan using common pantry ingredients. Keep the total under $80."

This kind of planning helps reduce impulse buys and last-minute takeout.

AI for Travel Planning

AI travel assistants like GuideGeek or prompts used in ChatGPT can:

- Build itineraries based on your interests
- Compare destinations or transport options
- Suggest restaurants and activities

Use Case: 3-Day Itinerary with Kids

Prompt:

"Plan a 3-day family trip to San Diego with two kids under 10. Include one educational stop, outdoor time, and meals near our hotel."

You'll get a formatted day-by-day itinerary with time slots and travel tips.

Follow-up prompt:

"Convert this into a Google Calendar format with times."

Use Case: Decision Support

Prompt:

"Compare Paris vs. Lisbon for a 5-day solo trip in September. Include cost, weather, language barrier, and walkability."

This kind of side-by-side prompt helps you decide based on lifestyle, not just cost.

AI for Daily and Weekly Reminders

Sometimes the most helpful AI feature is simply not forgetting.

Tools like Notion, Google Keep, Todoist, or AI-enhanced voice assistants (Siri, Alexa, Google Assistant) can generate structured checklists or send nudges based on prompts.

Use Case: Morning Routine Generator

Prompt:

"Create a 20-minute morning routine to improve focus and energy. Include hydration, light movement, and short journaling."

Follow-up prompt:

"Schedule this to repeat every weekday in my reminders app."

Use Case: Recurring Household Tasks

Prompt:

"Build a recurring weekly checklist for home tasks (laundry, trash, bills, meal prep). Add estimated time per task."

The AI will produce a simple list you can plug into any task manager.

Common Pitfalls to Avoid

- **Over-complicating prompts**: Keep it simple — ask for outcomes, not concepts
- **Too much automation**: Don't turn your life into a spreadsheet — use AI for relief, not rigidity
- **Skipping review**: Always sanity-check itineraries, recipes, or scheduling for feasibility

"AI should reduce stress, not increase your micromanagement."

Tactical Best Practices

- Use recurring prompt templates in a notes app
- Pair reminders with time-based triggers (e.g., after lunch)
- Store meal plans and itineraries in a shareable folder for reuse
- Use AI voice assistants to log tasks while multitasking
- Ask AI to include buffer time or prep time in schedules

Checklist: Smart Routines with AI

- Generate a realistic weekly meal plan
- Auto-create a categorized grocery list
- Build custom travel itineraries
- Compare travel destinations by lifestyle fit
- Schedule recurring routines and reminders

Real-World Example: Couple Saves 6+ Hours a Week on Planning

What happened: A busy couple used ChatGPT to:

- Create bi-weekly meal plans based on fridge inventory
- Auto-generate grocery lists linked to their favorite store app
- Plan weekend trips 2x/month with AI itineraries
- Schedule all home tasks in shared reminders

Result: Reduced decision fatigue, meal stress, and household disagreements. Gained back nearly a full workday of time each month.

What we learn: Small planning tasks — when optimized — make a big difference in mental space and household calm.

Conclusion

You don't need to outsource your life to AI — just the parts that feel like noise. With a few well-structured prompts and reliable tools, you can simplify meals, trips, and tasks without sacrificing control or personality.

The key is to stay human-led, AI-assisted.

Next Steps

Coming next: **AI for Mental Clarity: Journaling, Focus, & Habits** — where we look at how prompts can help you regain focus, reinforce goals, and track what really matters.

AI for Mental Clarity: Journaling, Focus, & Habits

Life moves fast. Thoughts pile up, to-do lists multiply, and good habits slip. But what if AI could help you slow the chaos — not by doing everything for you, but by helping you think more clearly, act more intentionally, and reflect more consistently?

This section explores how AI tools can support mental clarity: by guiding journaling, reinforcing focus habits, and tracking your goals. With the right prompts, you can use AI to clarify your thinking, not clutter it.

AI-Powered Journaling: Think Better on the Page

Journaling isn't just about keeping a diary — it's about making sense of what matters. With AI, you can:

- Generate thoughtful reflection prompts
- Turn scattered notes into structured entries
- Get summaries of your own thoughts over time

Use Case: Daily Guided Reflection

Prompt:

"Act as a journaling coach. Give me 3 questions to reflect on for today. Keep them short but meaningful."

Each day, this gives you a simple entry point into your thoughts — without the blank-page syndrome.

Follow-up prompt:

“Now summarize what I wrote into a 1-paragraph takeaway.”

Use Case: Mood and Pattern Tracking

Prompt:

“Based on my last 10 journal entries, summarize recurring emotions or themes. Suggest one positive action I can take.”

Over time, this turns journaling into insight — not just output.

AI for Focus and Distraction Recovery

Focus is under constant attack — messages, pings, tabs, interruptions. AI can help you:

- Block distractions with routines
- Create accountability for deep work
- Suggest ways to re-center after distraction

Use Case: Deep Work Routine Builder

Prompt:

“Design a 90-minute deep work session for writing a client proposal. Include warm-up, working blocks, and short breaks.”

Follow-up prompt:

“Schedule this into a calendar with reminders every 30 minutes.”

Use Case: Midday Reset Routine

Prompt:

"I've lost focus. Suggest a 10-minute reset routine to help me refocus, calm down, and restart productively."

These moments of recovery add up to serious gains in clarity.

Building Habits with AI Nudges and Logs

Habit formation is about consistency. AI can help reinforce behaviors with reminders, tracking, and check-ins.

Use Case: Creating a Habit Tracker in Notion or Sheets

Prompt:

"Build a 30-day habit tracker for exercise, journaling, and screen-free evenings. Add columns for streaks and notes."

Tools like Google Sheets or Notion can instantly turn this into a working system.

Use Case: Daily Habit Review Prompt

Prompt:

"At the end of each day, ask me if I did these 3 things: 30 min movement, no phone after 9pm, and wrote 1 paragraph of reflection. If not, suggest a way to reset tomorrow."

These gentle check-ins keep your momentum human, not robotic.

Mental Clarity Through Micro-Coaching

AI can also act as a lightweight, always-on coach. Whether you're making decisions, processing emotions, or untangling priorities, a simple prompt can provide perspective.

Use Case: Decision Clarity

Prompt:

"I'm stuck between two choices: switching jobs or staying. Help me evaluate both options with pros, cons, risks, and what matters most."

Follow-up prompt:

"Now reframe this decision as a values question. What does each option say about what I want most?"

Use Case: Mental Overload Release

Prompt:

"I'm feeling overwhelmed. Help me list out everything that's on my mind. Then group it into action, delay, delegate, or discard."

This exercise turns cognitive clutter into calm clarity.

Common Pitfalls to Avoid

- **Over-analyzing everything**: AI can help organize your thoughts — but only you can decide what matters.
- **Replacing emotion with logic**: Reflection tools should honor how you feel, not just what makes sense.
- **Using AI as a crutch**: Let AI prompt the questions, but make sure you're answering them honestly.

“AI isn’t your therapist — but it can be a very good mirror.”

Tactical Best Practices

- Save your favorite prompts in a quick-access file or app
- Use voice-to-text to journal on the go
- Set AI reminders to ask reflection questions at set times (e.g., bedtime)
- Export monthly summaries to track growth
- Ask AI to spot patterns in your own writing every 30 days

Checklist: Clarity, Focus, and Reflection

- Use AI to generate daily or weekly reflection prompts
- Build a focus routine with blocks and recovery time
- Track 2–3 habits in Sheets, Notion, or another favorite tool
- Run decision-making prompts when stuck
- Review journal themes monthly with AI-generated summaries

Real-World Example: Solo Founder Uses AI for Daily Reset

What happened: A solo startup founder felt pulled in too many directions. They started using ChatGPT for a 10-minute daily reflection at lunch.

What went right:

- Asked: “What’s most important for me to focus on this afternoon?”
- Reflected on the previous morning’s work
- Identified distractions and corrected them

Result: Regained 1–2 hours of productive time per day — with reduced stress and better end-of-day closure.

What we learn: Focus doesn't come from more hustle — it comes from intentional thinking. AI can prompt that without judgment.

Conclusion

Mental clarity isn't a luxury — it's the foundation of good decision-making, focus, and well-being. AI can't think for you, but it can give your thinking more structure, rhythm, and reflection.

When used with discipline, prompts and routines become a light mental scaffolding — helping you move through the day with purpose, not just productivity.

Next Steps

Next up: **Chapter 5: Content Creation with AI** — where we dive into how AI can help you write, design, record, and publish faster than ever — without sounding like a machine.

Chapter 5

Content Creation With AI

Blog Posts, Newsletters & Scripts with ChatGPT

Creating high-quality content — consistently and quickly — is one of the biggest challenges facing business owners, marketers, and creators today. Whether you're running a blog, sending a newsletter, or scripting a video or podcast, the demands never stop. But what if you could shorten the writing process by 60–80% without sacrificing clarity or voice?

This section shows how to leverage ChatGPT to generate, refine, and accelerate written content for your brand or business — while keeping it human, useful, and aligned with your goals.

Why AI Works for Content Creation

AI writing tools like ChatGPT are powerful because they:

- Understand structure and tone
- Respond to prompts quickly
- Provide variation and inspiration
- Reduce writer's block

But they don't replace your judgment — they amplify it. Used well, AI becomes your draft partner, brainstorming buddy, and structure coach.

Use Case: Blog Posts from Prompt to Publish

Let’s say you want to write a blog post titled: *"5 Ways Small Businesses Can Use AI Without Hiring a Developer."*

Step 1: Structure the Prompt

Prompt:

"Write a 1,000-word blog post titled '5 Ways Small Businesses Can Use AI Without Hiring a Developer'. Audience: small business owners. Tone: practical, friendly, non-technical. Include an intro, five clear sections, and a conclusion."

You’ll get a fully structured draft. But it’s just the start.

Step 2: Improve the Hook

Follow-up prompt:

“Rewrite the introduction to be more attention-grabbing and speak directly to overwhelmed small business owners.”

AI will adjust the tone and tighten the hook.

Step 3: Add Real Examples

Prompt:

“For point 3 in the post, add a real-world example of a local business using AI to automate customer emails.”

Step 4: Polish & Format

Prompt:

“Now convert this into a final blog format with subheadings, bullet points, and a call to action at the end.”

You can copy-paste this directly into your CMS or blog editor.

Use Case: Weekly Newsletter with Custom Sections

Newsletters are about building trust and delivering value. AI can help draft them faster while keeping your personal voice.

Step 1: Provide the Structure

Prompt:

"Write a weekly newsletter for my consulting audience. Theme: 'How to Use AI for Competitive Advantage'. Include: intro, quick tip, resource of the week, and one client story (fictional). Tone: expert, but friendly."

AI will return a full draft segmented into digestible blocks.

Step 2: Tune the Personal Tone

Prompt:

“Rewrite the client story to sound more like me telling it over coffee — casual but insightful.”

Follow-up prompt:

“Add a P.S. that invites replies with their own AI challenges.”

Use Case: Video or Podcast Scripts

AI can help structure scripts for:

- YouTube explainers
- Training videos
- Podcast intros/outros
- Ad reads or promos

Step 1: Start With a Hooked Script

Prompt:

"Write a 3-minute video script explaining how AI helps with content creation. Hook the viewer in the first 15 seconds. Include 3 main points and a clear outro with a call to action."

You get a draft with pacing, transitions, and clear narrative flow.

Step 2: Format for Readability

Prompt:

"Reformat this for a teleprompter — short sentences, no more than 12 words per line."

Follow-up prompt:

"Add pauses and emphasis cues (e.g., [pause], [emphasize]) for better delivery."

Common Pitfalls to Avoid

- **Letting AI write everything**: Your voice matters. Use AI for draft and structure — edit for personality.
- **Being too vague**: AI needs specifics — audience, format, goal, tone, and length.
- **Publishing without reviewing**: AI-generated content needs human insight. Always fact-check and revise.

“AI can write fast, but only you can write true.”

Tactical Best Practices

- Always specify your audience and purpose in prompts
- Use follow-up prompts to dial in tone, clarity, and flow
- Build reusable templates for blog intros, newsletter formats, and script outlines
- Save successful prompts in a swipe file
- Ask for 2–3 versions when exploring ideas — pick and mix the best parts

Checklist: Smarter Content Creation with ChatGPT

- Prompt with clear format, tone, and audience details
- Use follow-up prompts to tighten or enhance drafts
- Add real examples or case studies
- Format for the right platform (blog, email, script)
- Review, revise, and personalize before publishing

Real-World Example: Solo Marketer Saves 10 Hours per Week

What happened: A one-person marketing team for a boutique agency began using ChatGPT to draft all initial content — blog posts, weekly newsletters, and YouTube scripts.

What worked:

- Created a master prompt template
- Used AI for outlines, drafts, and formatting
- Spent time only on final voice and story polish

Result: Cut weekly writing time from 14 hours to just under 4 — while improving output quality and publishing cadence.

What we learn: Structure + prompts = sustainable content engine, even for lean teams.

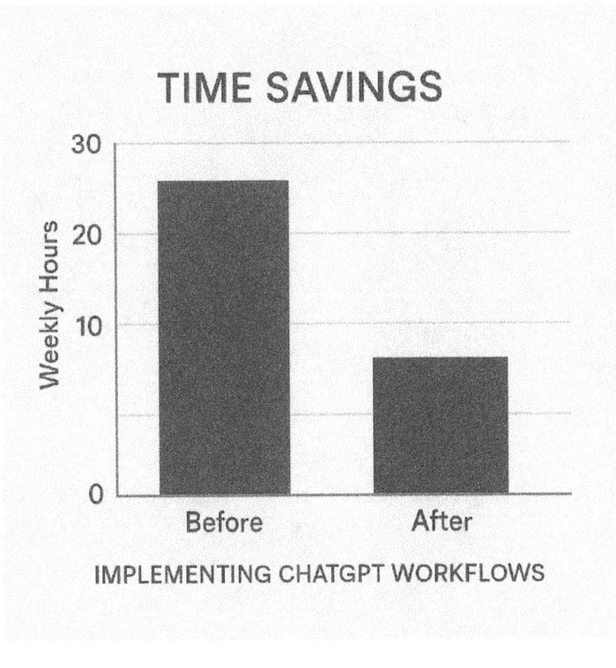

Bonus: Reuse and Repurpose AI Content

Prompt:

"Turn this blog post into:

- A LinkedIn post
- A 3-slide presentation outline
- A short email promo
- A podcast intro script"

You instantly get multi-channel content from a single idea.

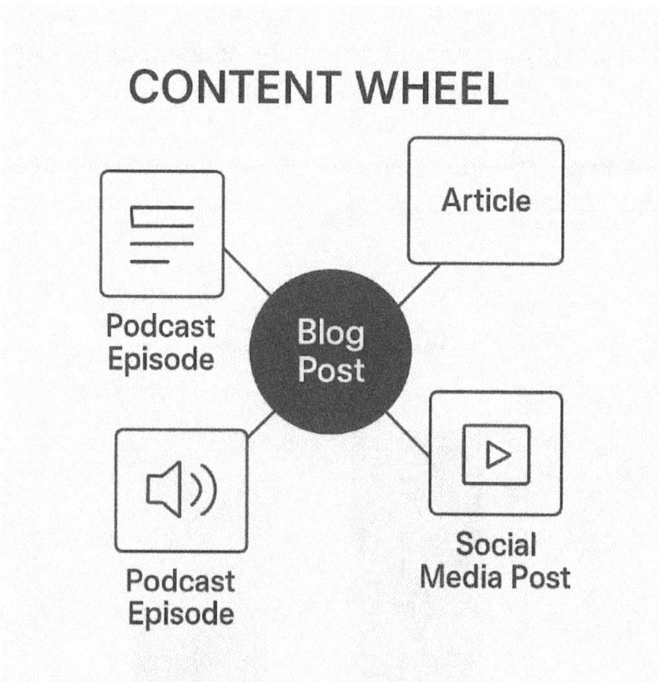

"Great content isn't written once — it's reshaped 5 different ways."

Conclusion

If writing feels like a bottleneck, it doesn't have to. With smart prompts and thoughtful editing, ChatGPT can help you create high-quality content faster than ever — and make room for what really matters: strategy, relationships, and consistency.

The more you prompt, test, and refine, the more it feels like your co-writer — not just a tool.

Next Steps

Coming next: **Social Captions & Hashtags with AI Optimization** — where we turn your message into scroll-stopping micro-content that actually gets noticed.

Social Captions & Hashtags with AI Optimization

Writing content is half the battle. Getting it seen is the rest. Social media demands speed, clarity, and relevance — often in under 280 characters. That's where AI thrives. With the right prompts, you can turn a blog post, offer, or insight into a headline-worthy caption, generate hashtags tuned to your niche, and adapt content across platforms without sounding robotic.

This section covers how to create scroll-stopping captions, intelligently match hashtags to your goals, and keep your brand voice sharp — all with AI.

Why AI Is a Game-Changer for Social Copy

Captions matter. But writing them well, and consistently, is time-consuming. AI tools like ChatGPT, Copy.ai, and Jasper are game-changers because they:

- Generate multiple variations quickly
- Adapt tone for different audiences or platforms
- Suggest optimized hashtags by theme or trend
- Let you repurpose content from blogs, newsletters, or videos

Used correctly, AI becomes a high-speed social content assistant — not a crutch.

Use Case: Turn a Blog Post Into 5 Captions

Let's say you wrote a blog titled, *"3 AI Tools That Save SMBs 10+ Hours a Week."*

Step 1: Summarize the Hook

Prompt:

"Write 5 social captions for LinkedIn based on this blog. Keep them short, hook-based, and relevant to time-strapped business owners. Include a soft call to action."

AI delivers:

- A punchy one-liner
- A stat-based hook
- A personal pain-point angle
- A story-driven lead-in
- A question format caption

Step 2: Add Hashtags

Prompt:

"Add 5 relevant, non-generic hashtags per caption. Focus on productivity, small business, and AI."

Follow-up:

"Now sort those hashtags by reach level: broad, mid, niche."

This creates a high-reach, high-fit tag strategy for each post.

Use Case: Platform-Specific Tweaks

Each platform has its own voice. AI helps adapt:

- LinkedIn: professional, value-driven
- Instagram: short, visual, engaging
- Twitter/X: snappy, threaded, conversation-starting
- Facebook: community-based, slightly longer

Prompt:

"Adapt this same message into:

- A LinkedIn post with a professional tone
- An Instagram caption with a conversational tone
- A Twitter thread starter (first tweet + hook)
- A Facebook post that includes a soft anecdote"

Use Case: Hashtag Discovery by Industry or Topic

Prompt:

"Generate 10 smart hashtags for a small business post about automating invoicing with AI. Group them by theme: tool, benefit, audience."

AI sorts them like this:

- **Tool**: #ZapierTips #AIautomation
- **Benefit**: #SaveTime #ScaleSmart
- **Audience**: #SmallBizLife #FounderTools

This beats generic bundles like #business or #tech.

Use Case: Timely or Trend-Based Captions

Prompt:

“Write a caption about time-saving AI tools tied to tax season. Audience: freelancers. Add urgency and value.”

Follow-up:

“Make it sound helpful, not gimmicky. Add a question to drive engagement.”

This keeps your content relevant to what people care about — now.

Common Pitfalls to Avoid

- **Overloading with hashtags**: Too many looks spammy. 5–8 per post is the sweet spot.
- **Using AI tone blindly**: Some tools default to bland or salesy copy — always tune it.
- **Hashtag stuffing**: Relevance beats reach. Niche hashtags connect better.

"The goal isn’t just impressions — it’s resonance."

Tactical Best Practices

- Prompt for 3–5 variations per caption — choose the strongest
- Use a prompt template for each platform
- Always include your post goal (click, share, comment, save)
- Ask AI to group or score hashtags by theme
- Save successful caption formats for reuse

Checklist: Social Copy with AI

- Convert blog or newsletter content into 3–5 social captions
- Adjust tone per platform (LinkedIn vs. Instagram vs. Twitter)
- Use 5–8 hashtags per post, sorted by theme or audience
- Add soft calls to action ("What do you think?", "Tag a friend")
- Store your best prompts and formats for reuse

Real-World Example: Boutique Brand Doubles Engagement in 2 Weeks

What happened: A solo founder used ChatGPT to repurpose her weekly blog into 4 LinkedIn posts and 3 Instagram captions.

What went right:

- Used format-specific prompts
- Added engagement hooks + hashtag clusters
- Tracked top-performing formats weekly

Result: Post engagement doubled — more likes, shares, and DMs — without adding hours of content work.

What we learn: Social content doesn't have to be original every day — just smartly adapted.

Conclusion

Social media isn't about constant originality — it's about clarity, consistency, and connection. With the right AI prompts, you can turn existing content into scroll-stopping captions that match your voice and reach the right people.

AI gives you the speed — your insight gives it meaning.

Next Steps

Coming next: **Designing Branded Graphics in Seconds with Canva AI** — how to create stunning visuals in your brand style using a few smart prompts and no design degree.

Designing Branded Graphics in Seconds with Canva AI

Strong visuals stop the scroll. But most business owners and content creators aren't designers — and they don't have time to spend hours learning design software or manually tweaking templates. That's where Canva's AI-powered tools step in: turning a few smart inputs into stunning, brand-consistent graphics.

Whether you need a LinkedIn carousel, Instagram story, YouTube thumbnail, or slide deck, Canva Magic tools dramatically speed up design while still keeping your look professional.

Why Visual Branding Matters (Even for Small Teams)

Visuals aren't fluff — they're clarity. The right graphic:

- Reinforces your message instantly
- Grabs attention without needing words
- Creates brand recognition over time
- Makes complex ideas more scannable and shareable

With Canva AI, you no longer need to outsource or stress. You can create on-brand visuals in minutes.

Use Case: Creating a LinkedIn Carousel in Minutes

Let's say you want to turn a blog post into a scrollable LinkedIn carousel.

Step 1: Start with Canva Magic Design

Prompt:

"Design a 5-slide LinkedIn carousel based on my blog post titled 'Top 3 AI Tools for SMB Efficiency.' Use a clean, modern look with bold headers and icons."

Magic Design instantly generates layout options with your content built-in.

Step 2: Brand It Fast with Styles

Click your saved brand kit or ask:

"Apply my brand colors and fonts from Acme Co. style guide."

The whole deck re-themes in seconds.

Use Case: Social Post Templates in Bulk

Prompt:

"Create 3 Instagram post templates promoting AI tips. Use my color palette and logo. Make sure one is good for quotes, one for stats, and one for short tips."

AI drafts layouts with varied visual structure while keeping the feel consistent.

Use Case: YouTube Thumbnail with AI-Picked Image and Text

Prompt:

"Design a YouTube thumbnail titled 'Zapier for Beginners'. Use bold text, tech color palette, and include a workflow-related icon."

Canva AI:

- Suggests layouts that work well in thumbnails
- Picks relevant imagery or generates it
- Auto-adjusts text for readability at small sizes

Magic Edit: Tweak Visuals Without Starting Over

Need to change just one thing?

- Swap a graphic
- Replace text with tone suggestions
- Reformat layout for a different platform

Prompt:

"Resize this carousel for Instagram Stories and adjust the font to be more playful."

Use Case: AI-Powered Presentation Decks

Prompt:

"Create a 7-slide presentation titled 'How AI Saves Time for Solopreneurs.' Add relevant visuals, keep text minimal, and match my brand style."

Magic Design lays out the entire deck, often better than most people would by hand.

Follow-up:

"Now add slide animations and export as video."

Common Pitfalls to Avoid

- **Overloading with effects**: Less is more. Let the design breathe.
- **Inconsistent branding**: Always apply your brand kit before exporting.
- **Too much text per visual**: Use AI to trim wording to visual-first formats.

"Your brand's visual tone is just as important as your written voice."

Tactical Best Practices

- Set up your brand kit in Canva first (colors, fonts, logo)
- Save 3–5 AI-generated templates per content type
- Use prompts with clarity: audience + use + style
- Keep layout formats consistent across platforms
- Reuse layouts with updated content weekly

Checklist: Design with Canva AI

- Set up brand kit in Canva
- Prompt Magic Design with your content and format
- Apply brand styling before finalizing
- Save templates by use case (carousel, story, reel, deck)
- Export for platform dimensions (1:1, 16:9, 9:16)

Real-World Example: Solo Consultant Launches with Polished Visuals

What happened: A solo consultant launching her brand used Canva Magic Design to build all her launch assets — 3 LinkedIn posts, a pitch deck, and a simple homepage graphic.

What went right:

- Used AI prompts to build layout ideas quickly
- Kept brand visuals consistent across platforms
- Saved and reused templates for future launches

Result: Built a launch presence in 1 day with no graphic designer.

What we learn: Canva AI gives non-designers the power to punch above their weight.

Conclusion

You don't need to be a designer — you need direction. With Canva AI, the magic is in how clearly you prompt and how consistently you apply your brand. It's visual content creation at speed and scale.

Next Steps

Coming up: **Repurposing Content with AI: From Text to Video** — turning your written insights into engaging video clips with just a few simple inputs.

Repurposing Content with AI: From Text to Video

Creating content from scratch is resource-intensive. But if you already have blogs, newsletters, podcasts, or even long-form social posts — you're sitting on a goldmine. With the right AI tools, you can transform those existing assets into compelling short-form videos, reels, explainers, or branded clips.

This section shows how to do just that: step-by-step, without expensive gear or production teams.

Why Repurpose? Why Video?

Because video drives reach.

- Social platforms prioritize it (Instagram, TikTok, LinkedIn)
- Audiences retain video better than text
- It humanizes your message

But the real reason? You've already done the hard work — crafting valuable ideas. AI just helps you bring them to life visually.

Tools That Make It Happen

Here are the top AI-driven tools for turning text into video:

- **Pictory**: Converts blog posts or scripts into narrated video with visuals and captions.
- **Synthesia**: Generates professional AI avatars and voiceovers — perfect for explainer-style content.
- **Lumen5**: Turns articles into animated slides with music and branding.
- **Descript**: Edits video like a document and can turn transcripts into new content.
- **InVideo**: Combines templates, stock footage, and AI narration for polished, editable results.

Use Case: Blog to YouTube Shorts with Pictory

You've got a blog titled "5 AI Hacks to Save 10 Hours a Week." Here's how to convert it.

Step 1: Import and Summarize

Prompt:

"Summarize this blog into 5 video points under 20 seconds each. Keep tone conversational, benefit-driven."

Step 2: Visualize and Narrate

Upload to Pictory. It auto-selects:

- Scene layout
- Relevant stock video
- On-screen text
- Voiceover (choose tone and gender)

Step 3: Brand and Export

Add your logo, color theme, music track, and CTA.

Use Case: AI Avatar Explainer with Synthesia

Let's say you're an accountant creating client onboarding content.

Prompt:

"Write a 90-second script explaining what a client can expect in their first 30 days. Use a friendly, reassuring tone."

Paste into Synthesia. Choose a human-like avatar, add your logo, and download the video for email or social.

Use Case: Social Reels from Podcast Audio

Take a recorded Zoom call or podcast clip.

Step 1: Use **Descript** to:

- Transcribe audio
- Remove filler words and pauses
- Highlight soundbites under 30 seconds

Step 2: Paste into **Lumen5** or **InVideo** to match visuals and format as vertical video.

Prompt:

"Create an Instagram Reel from this quote. Add kinetic text, relevant background, and light music. Keep under 30 seconds."

Prompt Frameworks for Video Repurposing

Here are reusable structures you can copy:

Prompt for explainer video:

"Turn this blog post into a 1-minute explainer script. Start with a hook, break into 3 parts, end with a strong CTA."

Prompt for short-form clip:

"Extract 3 key lines from this article to use as a social reel script. Keep it snappy and visual."

Prompt for narrator tone:

"Make the script sound casual and upbeat. Write as if speaking to a friend who runs a small business."

Common Pitfalls to Avoid

- **Trying to convert everything**: Focus on evergreen, outcome-driven pieces.
- **Using robotic narration**: Humanize tone or use a realistic AI avatar.
- **Skipping captions**: Many users scroll without sound. Always include text.
- **Overcomplicating visuals**: Simpler is often more watchable on mobile.

Tactical Best Practices

- Keep clips under 60 seconds unless for long-form YouTube
- Always start with a hook in the first 3 seconds
- Match visuals to the *emotion* of your message, not just keywords
- Batch-produce 3–5 videos from one article or transcript
- Use the same brand kit across tools (colors, logos, outro)

Checklist: Text to Video Workflow

- Pick a strong blog, newsletter, or long post
- Break it into 3–5 video points
- Choose format: explainer, avatar, reel, story, etc.
- Prompt for script tone and CTA
- Use Pictory/Synthesia/Lumen5 to visualize and brand
- Add captions, music, and export

Real-World Example: Consultant Turns Blog Library Into Client Leads

What happened: A solo consultant had 20 blog posts that weren't driving traffic. They used Pictory and Lumen5 to convert them into short-form explainer videos and post weekly.

What went right:

- Created a pipeline: Blog → Video → Social + Email
- Used AI to speed up voiceover and visual matching
- Kept videos short, clear, and brand-aligned

Result: Saw a 4x increase in profile views and inbound consultation requests within 8 weeks.

What we learn: Video visibility extends the life and reach of written insight.

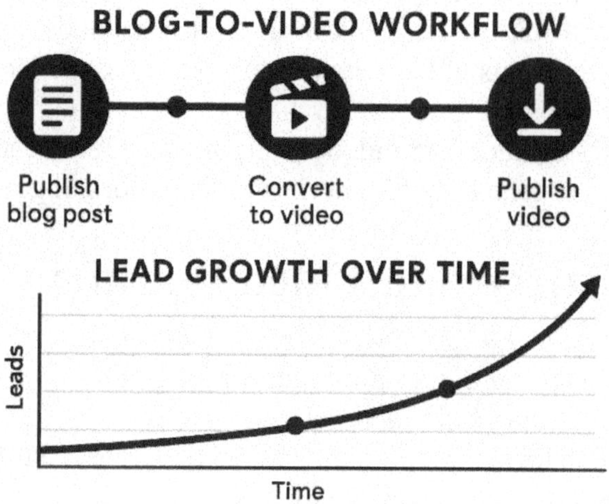

Conclusion

Text is valuable. But video reaches further. With AI tools like Pictory, Lumen5, Synthesia, and Descript, any article, transcript, or even long-form caption becomes a dynamic visual asset.

Don't reinvent the wheel. Just press record — with the words you already have.

Next Steps

Coming up: **Ethics: Avoiding Plagiarism and Watermark Detection** — how to use AI-generated media responsibly, and what to watch for in detection tools.

Ethics: Avoiding Plagiarism and Watermark Detection

As generative AI becomes a go-to tool for content creation, it introduces new risks — especially around ownership, attribution, and hidden markers left behind in what you publish. SMB leaders and content creators must not only know *how* to use AI, but *how to use it responsibly.*

In this section, we break down what you must know about AI plagiarism risks, watermark detection, and ethical safeguards that protect your credibility and your brand.

What Counts as Plagiarism with AI?

You may not be copying text manually — but that doesn't mean you're safe from duplicate content risks. AI-generated text can unintentionally resemble existing published work, especially when based on highly saturated prompts.

Common forms of unintentional AI plagiarism:

- Verbatim copying of well-known phrases or definitions
- Generated content that mirrors existing articles or blog structures
- Content that rephrases someone else's opinion too closely without attribution

Prompt example that leads to risk:

"Write an article about the benefits of remote work."

That's too generic — and the output might closely match existing content across the web.

Watermarks: What Are They and Why Should You Care?

Watermarks are invisible markers embedded in images, audio, or video generated by some AI tools. These help platforms trace content back to its origin — for detection, moderation, or legal review.

Examples of watermarking systems:

- OpenAI inserts cryptographic markers in some image outputs
- Google's SynthID tags AI-generated media with invisible digital fingerprints
- Shutterstock and Adobe Firefly watermark generated stock

If your business uses AI-generated assets in ads, print, or client work, you need to:

- Check for embedded watermarks
- Avoid violating TOS by reselling or redistributing without license
- Credit appropriately when required

Detection Tools Are Getting Smarter

Even if you edit AI text slightly, detection tools are catching up. Institutions, search engines, and platforms increasingly use classifiers to detect AI-authored content.

Tools that analyze AI-origin:

- GPTZero: Detects AI-written essays and content
- Turnitin AI Detection: Used by universities
- Originality.ai: Detects AI content in blogs, marketing, and web copy

If flagged, content can be demoted, rejected, or cause credibility issues — especially for client work or public publishing.

Best Practices to Stay Clear

Here's how to generate smart, safe, and original content using AI.

1. Use Personalization in Prompts

The more unique your input, the less likely your output will resemble someone else's.

Prompt: "Write 3 benefits of remote work based on my company's experience managing a 12-person hybrid team in consulting."

2. Always Review and Rework

Don't publish AI output as-is. Edit, add human insight, restructure.

- Reorder bullet points
- Add analogies from your business
- Include custom examples or phrasing

3. Check with Detection Tools First

If publishing content professionally or at scale, run it through a plagiarism or AI detection scanner.

- Originality.ai for content marketers
- Copyscape or Grammarly for general plagiarism

4. Keep Records of Your Inputs

If you use AI for client work, archive the original prompts and your edits. This helps prove authorship and intent.

5. Attribute Where Needed

When using AI to summarize or rephrase published ideas, credit the original source:

"Based on ideas from Harvard Business Review's 2023 article on remote work culture."

Real-World Example: Freelancer Flagged for Duplicate Blog

What happened: A freelance writer used AI to generate a blog post for a client. The client uploaded it to their CMS, but their SEO plugin flagged 80% similarity to an existing HubSpot article.

What went wrong:

- Used a generic prompt with no brand-specific context
- Published with minimal editing
- Didn't check for similarity before delivery

What we learn:

- AI plagiarism isn't always intentional
- Detection tools are now embedded into business software
- Brand trust is easy to lose with duplicate content

Fix:

- Add unique brand voice layers
- Reorganize layout and argument structure
- Credit source if paraphrasing from research

Common Pitfalls to Avoid

- **Assuming AI text is always unique** — it's not
- **Using generic prompts** — they increase duplication risk
- **Skipping editing** — humanize and restructure every time
- **Overusing public datasets** — especially for regulated content (health, finance, legal)

Tactical Best Practices

- Always run AI-generated long-form through detection tools
- Layer personal or brand anecdotes on top of AI base drafts
- Avoid copying tone, layout, or structure from known publishers
- Prompt with specifics: who you are, what you do, what your reader needs
- Know which tools watermark outputs before you use them in commercial settings

Checklist: Ethical AI Use for Content

- Add business-specific detail in every prompt
- Always edit and restructure before publishing
- Run detection scan for public or client-facing content
- Track your original prompts for accountability
- Credit any referenced work or insight

Conclusion

Smart AI use goes beyond speed — it's about trust. By embedding ethics into how you prompt, write, and publish, you protect your brand, your reputation, and your long-term visibility.

Next Steps

Coming up: **Chapter 6 — AI for Work and Productivity**: From inbox management to workflows and team collaboration, we explore where AI truly shines in day-to-day operations.

Chapter 6

AI for Work & Productivity

Inbox Zero with Gmail AI & Smart Filters

Email overwhelm isn't just a productivity issue — it's a security risk, a workflow bottleneck, and a source of daily stress for leaders and teams alike. But today's AI-powered inboxes can do more than autocomplete responses or flag spam. Gmail, in particular, now includes smart filters, AI-based suggestions, and integrations that help SMBs actually reach (and maintain) Inbox Zero.

In this section, we walk through how to reclaim your inbox using Gmail's native AI tools — with zero coding, minimal setup, and maximum payoff.

The Real Cost of Inbox Overload

Every minute you spend triaging email is time not spent on high-value work. Missed emails create client delays. Poor categorization leads to lost information. A cluttered inbox becomes:

- A liability during audits
- A blocker for quick decisions
- A mental drain on team focus

Getting to Inbox Zero isn't about deleting everything — it's about *trusting* your system to catch, file, or auto-handle what matters.

Gmail AI Features That Work for You

Google has embedded powerful AI capabilities into Gmail. You're likely already using some — but here's how to take full advantage:

Smart Compose

- Autocomplete full phrases based on your writing style
- Learns over time from your past messages
- Reduces typing time by 30–50% for frequent replies

Smart Reply

- Suggests 1-click responses based on tone/context
- Works well for short acknowledgments, quick decisions

Priority Inbox

- Automatically sorts emails into: *Primary, Social, Promotions, Updates*
- Learns what's important based on your behavior

Nudges

- AI reminds you to follow up on emails you've ignored
- Resurfaces important threads at just the right time

Search Chips and Filters

- Suggests auto-filters when you search (e.g., "has attachment," "from client," "before 2023")
- Filters can be saved to automate future organization

Real-World Workflow: AI-Enhanced Client Inbox

Scenario: A marketing agency manages 20+ clients via Gmail. Without a system, critical updates got buried.

Solution:

1. **Set up labels** by client name
2. **Create filters**: If email contains subject "[ClientName]" or from specific domain → apply label, mark as important
3. **Enable priority inbox** with primary focused only on labeled clients
4. **Use Smart Reply** for common questions: "Approved," "Scheduled," "Please send next steps."

Result: 3 hours saved weekly per team member.

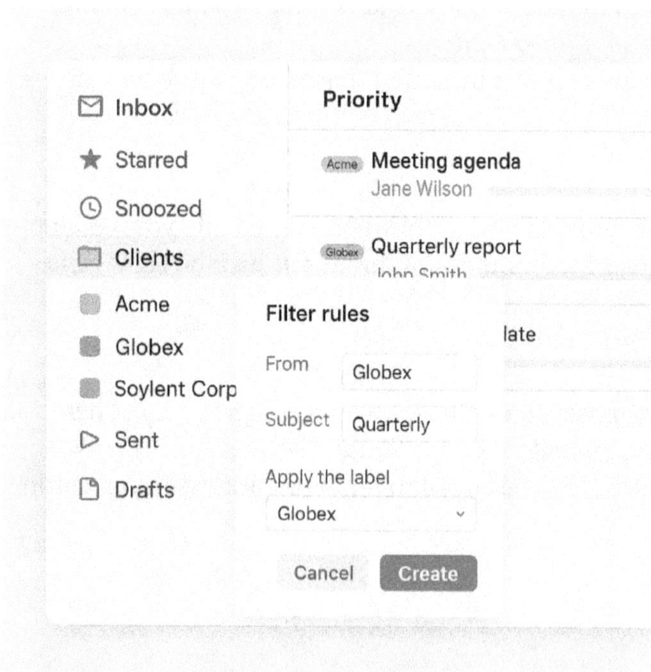

How to Create Smart Filters in Gmail

Step-by-step:

1. In Gmail, click the **filter icon** in the search bar
2. Set criteria: from, subject line, words, date, etc.
3. Click **Create filter**
4. Choose action: apply label, skip inbox, star, forward
5. Optional: Apply to past emails

Use filters like:

- From: invoices@domain.com → label "Finance"
- Subject includes "weekly report" → mark important
- From:@linkedin.com → archive automatically

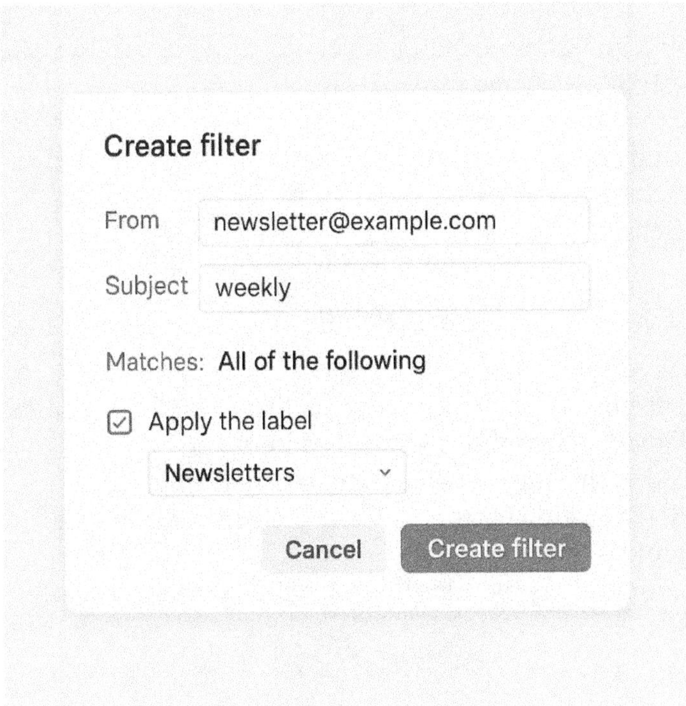

Prompt-Based Email Triage with Google Workspace + Gemini

If your Workspace account includes **Google Gemini**, here's how to use AI prompting to speed up inbox triage:

Prompt:

"Summarize the last 10 unread emails in this thread. Flag anything needing action this week."

Prompt:

"Generate a 3-bullet response to this inquiry using our last sent quote as reference."

Gemini integrates into Gmail natively for eligible accounts and offers sidebar assistance for:

- Drafting
- Summarizing
- Decision support

Tactical Best Practices

- Unsubscribe in bulk: Use tools like Clean Email or leave it to Gmail's "Unsubscribe" suggestions
- Mark phishing or spam to train Gmail's detection
- Set "vacation responder" with AI-generated language for professionalism
- Group filters by role (finance, HR, sales) for teams

Common Pitfalls to Avoid

- **Over-filtering**: Important messages may skip inbox entirely
- **Neglecting label maintenance**: Review every 2–3 months
- **Relying solely on Smart Reply**: Always customize for clients
- **Not training your inbox**: Every skip, star, or reply improves Gmail's AI

Checklist: Reaching Inbox Zero with AI

- Enable Smart Compose and Smart Reply
- Use at least 5 smart filters and labels
- Activate Priority Inbox or split tabs
- Schedule 2 triage windows daily (15 mins each)
- Use Gemini or summaries to speed decisions
- Archive instead of delete — searchable later

Real-World Example: Startup Founder Reclaims 5 Hours/Week

What happened: A founder received 200+ emails/day — investor threads, product updates, user support, and marketing junk.

What worked:

- Created filters for "Investor" and "Support"
- Smart Reply used for investor check-ins
- Gemini used to summarize team update threads into daily digest

Result: Cut inbox time from 90 minutes/day to 30.

UNFILTERED INBOX	AI-ENHANCED WORKFLOW
Emails received this week **245**	Emails received this week **245**
Hours spent on email this week **12**	Categorized by AI **210**
	Prompts sent by AI **35**
	Hours spent on email this week **5**

Conclusion

AI can't delete your emails — but it can *teach your inbox* to work for you. Whether you're a solo operator or a team juggling 50 threads, Gmail's smart tools reduce friction, protect focus, and support rapid action.

Next Steps

Coming up: **AI Meeting Notes & Summaries (Otter, Fireflies)** — how to stop taking notes manually and let AI capture what matters in every meeting.

AI Meeting Notes & Summaries (Otter, Fireflies)

In the modern business world, time isn't just money — it's momentum. Every meeting, whether it's a client update, a team sync, or a strategic discussion, carries decisions, insights, and next steps. But far too often, those key takeaways vanish the moment the call ends. Enter AI-powered meeting tools like Otter.ai and Fireflies — not just digital note-takers, but real-time strategic assets for businesses looking to reduce friction, boost accountability, and unlock post-meeting productivity.

This section breaks down how to use AI note-takers to transform the way your team handles meetings, with tactical walkthroughs, best practices, and tools anyone can implement — no tech degree required.

Why Traditional Note-Taking Doesn't Scale

Manual notes slow down participation, drain attention, and introduce bias. Everyone captures different pieces. Few people revisit the full context. Key points are lost.

Common issues in manual note-taking:

- Incomplete records
- Missed action items
- Delayed follow-ups
- He-said-she-said confusion on decisions

With AI note-taking, none of this depends on human memory. Tools like Otter and Fireflies listen, transcribe, summarize, and even tag decisions automatically.

What AI Meeting Tools Actually Do

At their core, tools like Otter and Fireflies:

- Transcribe speech into searchable text
- Identify and tag speakers
- Summarize conversations into bullet points
- Auto-detect tasks, decisions, and key phrases
- Sync with calendar tools (Zoom, Google Meet, MS Teams)

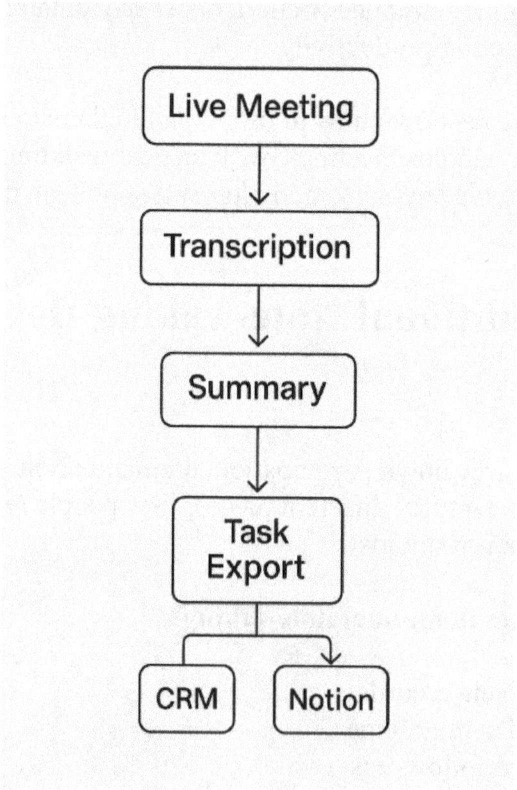

Otter.ai: Best for Real-Time Collaboration and Teams

Otter is ideal for SMBs and remote teams who want real-time access to meeting insights.

Key Features:

- Live transcription shared during the meeting
- Automatic speaker identification
- Highlight and comment features during transcription
- Integrates with Zoom, Google Meet, Teams
- OtterPilot: Automatically joins scheduled calls, transcribes, summarizes

Use Case:
A distributed design team holds three weekly product meetings. Otter:

- Automatically joins based on Google Calendar
- Records, transcribes, and posts a live doc to shared Google Drive
- Email summaries sent 10 minutes after call ends

Bonus: Users can click on any sentence in the transcript and hear the exact moment it was said.

Fireflies.ai: Best for Action-Driven Teams and CRM Sync

Fireflies focuses more on actionable insights and team productivity post-call.

Key Features:

- Automated call recording & transcription
- Smart search (filter by speaker, keyword, sentiment)
- Auto-detection of tasks, deadlines, commitments
- Integrates with CRMs like Salesforce, HubSpot
- Slack, Trello, Notion, Asana integrations

Use Case:
A small sales agency uses Fireflies to:

- Auto-record sales calls
- Extract tasks and objections
- Sync notes to CRM
- Trigger follow-up emails using Zapier automation

Otter vs. Fireflies: Feature Comparison

Feature	Otter.ai	Fireflies.ai
Real-time transcription	✅	❌ (post-meeting only)
Speaker identification	✅	✅
CRM Integration	❌	✅
Task & sentiment extraction	❌	✅
Collaboration (comments)	✅	✅
Calendar auto-join	✅	✅

Best Practices for AI Meeting Summaries

1. Set naming conventions
Use calendar tags like [CLIENT], [INTERNAL], [DEMO] to label transcripts.

2. Prep participants
Notify team/clients that AI is present. Transparency builds trust.

3. Train on usage
Ensure team knows how to:

- Highlight key sections
- Export tasks
- Comment and assign inside transcripts

4. Sync to your workspace
Push summaries to Notion, Google Docs, or Slack.

5. Regularly audit accuracy
Especially for proper nouns, technical terms, and action detection.

Common Pitfalls

- **Over-relying on AI summaries**: Always review full transcripts for nuance
- **Skipping edits**: Clean up summaries before sharing externally
- **Forgetting to manage permissions**: Private calls can be accidentally shared
- **Using vague meeting names**: Makes transcript search harder

Tactical Checklist: AI Meeting Mastery

- Connect AI tool to calendar
- Standardize meeting titles
- Notify participants of AI usage
- Tag follow-ups during review
- Export and assign tasks in project management tool
- Review summaries before archiving

Real-World Example: Fractional COO Running 5+ Weekly Teams

What happened: A fractional COO ran 5–7 weekly check-ins across HR, Ops, Finance, and Marketing for multiple clients. Manually writing summaries took 5+ hours/week.

What worked:

- Otter joined calls via Google Calendar
- Each summary was exported to shared Notion workspaces
- Tasks were tagged with @ mentions during transcript review
- Clients got recap links 15 mins post-meeting

Result: Saved 6 hours weekly, improved delegation clarity, and reduced repeat conversations.

Strategic Impact

- **Faster project execution**: No waiting for meeting notes
- **Improved accountability**: Every decision traceable
- **Easier onboarding**: New hires can review past transcripts
- **Cross-timezone alignment**: Asynchronous collaboration

Advanced Tips

Use sentiment tagging (Fireflies)
Identify emotional tone in sales/client calls

Embed meeting links in your CRM
Link exact discussion to client or deal record

Create a searchable archive
Use Otter's keyword tagging for repeat themes (e.g. "Q3 roadmap")

Prompt AI summaries with custom templates

"Summarize by team, action items, and blockers."

Conclusion

AI tools like Otter and Fireflies aren't just a luxury — they're a leverage point. When used correctly, they don't just save time — they sharpen memory, streamline teamwork, and close the loop between what's said and what gets done.

Next Steps

Coming up: **Task Automation Without Coding (Zapier + Notion AI)** — how to turn recurring work into autopilot systems using smart, no-code workflows.

Task Automation Without Coding (Zapier + Notion AI)

When small and mid-sized businesses talk about scaling, they often mean doing more without hiring more. That makes automation one of the most valuable strategic levers a business can pull. But for non-technical teams, building automation used to mean hiring developers or settling for rigid off-the-shelf solutions.

Not anymore. Today, tools like Zapier and Notion AI make task automation possible — and practical — for anyone who can click, drag, and type. These platforms allow you to eliminate repetitive tasks, reduce error-prone handoffs, and make systems work smarter without writing a single line of code.

This section will walk you through how to start automating common business tasks with Zapier and Notion AI, even if you're starting from scratch.

What No-Code Automation Really Means

No-code tools let you create logic-driven workflows using visual interfaces instead of programming languages. With Zapier and Notion AI, you can:

- Connect different apps you already use (email, calendar, CRM, task manager)
- Set triggers ("when this happens...") and actions ("do this")
- Schedule or delay tasks automatically
- Summarize, clean, or reformat data

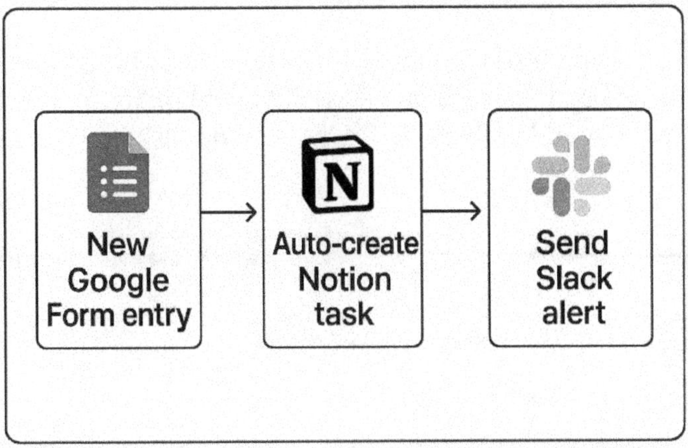

This means you can:

- Create new leads in Notion when someone fills out a form
- Post social content at the best time without manual clicks
- Send onboarding emails to new clients automatically

Zapier: The Workflow Connector

Zapier is one of the most widely used no-code automation platforms. It connects over 6,000+ apps with prebuilt "Zaps" that trigger actions.

How it works:

1. Choose a **Trigger** (e.g. new row in Google Sheets)
2. Choose an **Action** (e.g. create new Trello card)
3. Optional: add logic (e.g. only if amount > $100)

Common SMB automations:

- New Typeform response → Create lead in Pipedrive
- Stripe payment received → Send client onboarding email
- New Gmail label "Follow-Up" → Add task in Todoist

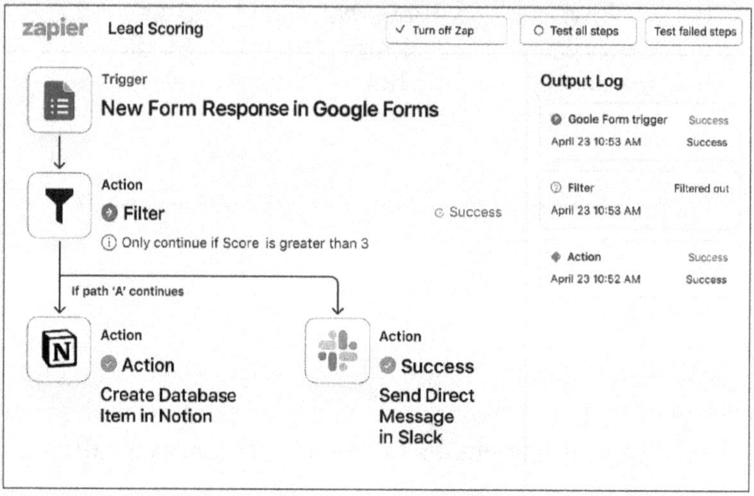

Notion AI: Your Smart Assistant Inside Notion

Notion AI enhances the Notion workspace by adding natural language tools to summarize, draft, analyze, and generate content. Paired with Zapier, it becomes a dynamic automation hub.

How SMBs use Notion AI:

- Automatically summarize meeting notes pasted from Otter
- Auto-generate blog outlines based on prompts
- Draft follow-up emails using task history
- Rewrite CRM notes into client-ready summaries

Example workflow:

1. Fireflies ends meeting → sends notes to Notion
2. Notion AI summarizes transcript → flags action items
3. Zapier adds flagged tasks to Asana and assigns based on tags

Combining Zapier + Notion AI: Power in Tandem

Alone, each tool is useful. Together, they're a compounding productivity engine.

Example 1: Content Pipeline

- Google Form: "Suggest blog topic" → New Notion row
- Notion AI drafts 5-point outline → Editor reviews
- Final post moves to "Ready" → Zapier schedules social posts

Example 2: Sales CRM Updates

- Calendly booking confirmed → Zapier logs event in Notion
- Post-call, Otter sends transcript to Notion
- Notion AI generates follow-up email
- Zapier sends it via Gmail using template

Real-World Example: Law Office Admin Saves 10 Hours/Week

What happened: A legal admin was spending time:

- Moving intake form data into Notion manually
- Sending emails to confirm appointments
- Tagging lawyers for document prep

What worked:

- Zapier used to pull in intake data automatically
- Email confirmations triggered when "status" changed
- Notion AI created task checklists per case type

Result: Saved over 10 hours weekly and reduced intake errors.

Actionable Use Cases for SMBs

1. Lead Management

- Trigger: New lead via Facebook/Typeform
- Action: Add to Notion CRM, send Slack alert, schedule email

2. Client Onboarding

- Trigger: Invoice paid in Stripe
- Action: Create client folder in Google Drive, send welcome packet, assign kickoff task

3. Recurring Weekly Reports

- Trigger: Every Monday at 9 AM
- Action: Create Notion page, summarize tasks from last week, assign reviews

Tactical Best Practices

- **Use Zapier Paths**: Add if/then logic to make flows dynamic
- **Test before going live**: Always run test records in Zapier
- **Label your Zaps clearly**: "Client_Onboarding_Email" is better than "Zap #3"
- **Audit regularly**: Review automations monthly to retire or update

Common Mistakes to Avoid

- **Over-automating**: Don't remove all human checkpoints, especially in legal/finance
- **Forgetting permissions**: Make sure Zapier has access to right Notion databases
- **Neglecting error logs**: Zapier will silently fail if fields mismatch — check logs weekly

Checklist: Getting Started with No-Code Automation

- Create a free Zapier account
- Identify 3 repetitive tasks you do weekly
- Build 1 simple 2-step Zap to start
- Enable Notion AI (on Plus plan or higher)
- Test auto-summarization with meeting notes
- Connect Notion to Zapier securely (use workspace token)

Conclusion

You don't need to be technical to build automated systems. You need to understand your workflows, choose the right triggers, and let AI + logic do the rest. Whether it's cutting down meeting follow-ups, simplifying onboarding, or keeping projects flowing without manual nudges — task automation gives you back time and control.

Coming up next: **Planning Projects with AI-Powered Tools** — using smart assistants, templates, and dashboards to manage deadlines, deliverables, and team coordination in real time.

Planning Projects with AI-Powered Tools

Effective project planning has long been a balance of managing deadlines, delegating work, and tracking progress. But for busy professionals—especially in small to mid-sized businesses—traditional planning methods often fall short. They're too manual, too rigid, or simply not built for the fast pace of modern work.

Fortunately, a new class of tools is rewriting the rulebook. AI-powered project management platforms now enable teams to plan smarter, faster, and with greater flexibility. These platforms integrate natural language inputs, automate updates, and even suggest timelines, helping you stay ahead without getting buried in details.

This section explores how SMBs can use AI-powered tools to break free of outdated planning habits and adopt workflows that adapt to how people actually work.

Why AI Is Changing Project Management

Traditional project tools require constant upkeep. You manually input task descriptions, assign team members, update timelines, and chase status reports. AI-powered tools flip the script by:

- Generating task lists from plain-English prompts
- Assigning due dates based on historical patterns and current workload
- Summarizing updates and identifying roadblocks automatically
- Providing visual dashboards that adjust in real time

The biggest advantage? Context-awareness. AI doesn't just help you store project info—it understands it and acts on it.

Top Tools for AI-Driven Project Planning

Notion with AI

Notion combines docs, task lists, calendars, databases, and team communication. Its built-in AI assistant now lets you:

- Generate project timelines from a simple description
- Summarize meeting notes and extract tasks
- Convert rough outlines into structured to-do lists
- Use natural language to manage updates across a project board

Best for: Cross-functional teams and creative planning workflows.

ClickUp AI

ClickUp is a project management platform with deeply integrated AI capabilities. Teams can:

- Draft subtasks automatically
- Rewrite vague task names into actionable descriptions
- Auto-summarize project updates for weekly reports
- Suggest assignees based on availability

Best for: Teams with tight deadlines and large task volumes.

Motion

Motion uses AI to plan your calendar based on project needs, priority, and workload.

- Schedules tasks automatically to optimize for deadlines
- Reschedules meetings if something higher-priority comes up
- Helps balance deep work vs. meetings

Best for: Professionals with lots of back-to-back commitments.

Real-World Case Study: Streamlining a Product Launch

The problem: A startup team of four was launching a new SaaS feature. They struggled to coordinate tasks, manage dependencies, and keep the release on track.

What they did:

- Wrote a 3-paragraph project brief in Notion
- Used Notion AI to extract tasks, assign dates, and suggest phases
- Integrated their calendar with Motion to schedule work blocks automatically
- Used ClickUp AI to auto-generate end-of-week summaries

Results:

- Cut planning time by 80%
- Finished feature 10 days ahead of schedule
- Saved ~20 hours per team member during the sprint

Department-Specific Use Cases

Marketing

- Prompt AI to create launch plans, press timelines, and social media calendars
- Auto-generate creative briefs based on campaign goals
- Summarize analytics and adjust planning in real time

HR & Operations

- Create onboarding plans from a new hire's job description
- Automate check-in tasks, goal setting, and performance reviews
- Summarize employee feedback from surveys into reports

Product & Engineering

- Auto-prioritize bug tickets by frequency and impact
- Use AI to summarize sprint reviews
- Generate task lists from user feedback collected in Notion or Airtable

Tactical Best Practices

- **Use AI Templates**: Most tools offer prompt-based templates like "Plan a marketing campaign" or "Create onboarding checklist." Customize and reuse.
- **Break Work into Phases**: AI works best when it understands structure. Define clear phases like Research, Development, QA, and Launch.
- **Review Before Assigning**: Always review and edit what AI generates. It can guess wrong—use your judgment.
- **Create Recurring Auto-Reports**: Set AI to send summaries each Friday so your team always knows what's next.

Common Mistakes and How to Avoid Them

Mistake 1: Expecting Perfection
AI will get close—but not perfect. Treat its outputs as drafts, not gospel.

Mistake 2: Too Many Tools
Don't use five platforms when two will do. Stick to one task planner and one dashboarding tool.

Mistake 3: Over-Automating
Human review is still essential. Don't let AI assign critical tasks without oversight.

Checklist: Build Your First AI-Powered Plan

- Choose a tool (Notion, ClickUp, or Motion)
- Draft a plain-English brief: "We need to redesign the homepage by next month"
- Use AI to generate a timeline and to-do list
- Review task suggestions and adjust for accuracy
- Assign roles and connect calendars or Slack
- Schedule weekly auto-summaries or check-ins

What Success Looks Like

Before: Endless email threads, forgotten deadlines, and fragmented plans.

After: A single dashboard shows:

- What's been done
- What's due next
- What's blocked (and why)
- Who's responsible

Conclusion

Project planning isn't about Gantt charts anymore—it's about giving your team the clarity and autonomy to execute. AI-powered tools remove friction, reduce planning fatigue, and surface insights that would otherwise be buried in status updates.

Even if you're new to structured planning, tools like Notion AI, ClickUp, and Motion make it feel less like managing and more like collaborating—with a virtual assistant who never forgets anything.

Coming up next: **Creating Reports & Presentations with ChatGPT & Canva** — where you'll learn how to turn raw ideas, notes, or spreadsheets into boardroom-ready assets in minutes.

Creating Reports & Presentations with ChatGPT & Canva

Reports and presentations are the backbone of decision-making in any organization. But creating them manually—especially under time pressure—can drain your team's attention and delay the real work: action and execution.

This is where AI tools like ChatGPT and Canva step in. Used together, they don't just save time—they radically improve how you turn raw data into clear, polished deliverables that drive decisions. Whether it's a monthly update for stakeholders or a pitch deck for a new client, these tools help you go from draft to delivery in a fraction of the time.

Let's explore how.

Why This Matters for SMBs

In a small or mid-sized business, you often don't have a team of analysts or designers. The same person writing the sales report might be running the next team meeting. And unlike large enterprises, there's no buffer for poor communication. If your report or deck isn't clear, the whole business slows down.

AI removes bottlenecks by:

- Drafting structured summaries from messy notes
- Suggesting clear visuals to match data
- Laying out presentations without a design background

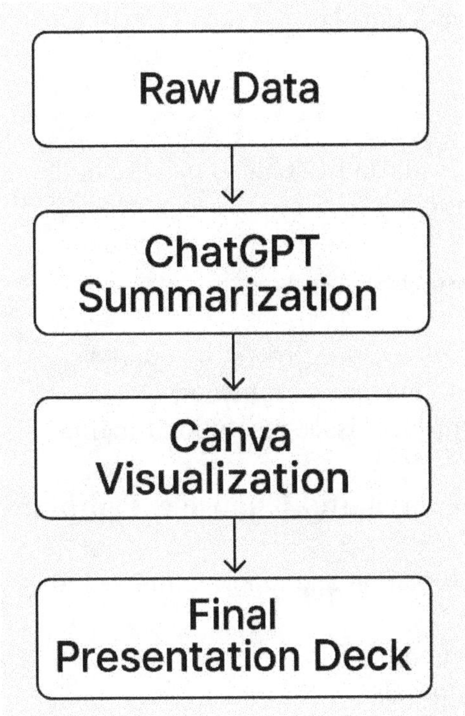

Step-by-Step: From Idea to Presentation

Step 1: Generate a Draft in ChatGPT

Start with a simple prompt like:

"Write a quarterly sales report for a SaaS startup with a 15% revenue increase, noting 2 product issues and 3 customer wins. Keep it concise and executive-friendly."

ChatGPT will deliver a rough draft with:

- Executive summary
- Key metrics
- Notable wins and issues
- Suggested next steps

Step 2: Ask for Visuals

Follow up with:

"List suggested charts and visuals to include in the report. Include short descriptions."

ChatGPT might suggest:

- Bar chart of revenue growth by quarter
- Pie chart of customer segments
- Table of product issue resolution timelines

Step 3: Open Canva and Choose a Template

Canva offers presentation and report templates for:

- Financial updates
- Client proposals
- Marketing reports
- Strategic plans

Import your text and match visuals based on ChatGPT's suggestions.

Step 4: Use Canva's Magic Design and Chart Tools

Use Canva's Magic Design AI to:

- Auto-format your layout
- Suggest visual themes based on your topic
- Resize for different outputs (slides, PDFs, social media)

For charts:

- Paste your data or ask ChatGPT to generate dummy data
- Let Canva convert them into visuals (bar, pie, line, table)

Real-World Example: Executive Report in 2 Hours

Scenario: A solo founder needs to send a monthly investor update. Previously took 8 hours across a weekend.

New process:

1. Copies rough bullet points from Notion
2. Pastes them into ChatGPT with a clear prompt
3. Gets a polished draft in 30 minutes
4. Opens Canva, selects a simple update template
5. Uses Magic Design to auto-layout text and insert charts

Time saved: 6 hours
Result: Clean, professional report sent before Monday

Tactical Use Cases for Reports and Decks

Client-Facing Work

- Create branded proposals and pitch decks
- Summarize discovery calls into actionable recommendations
- Visualize timelines and deliverables

Internal Comms

- Departmental updates for all-hands
- Project post-mortems and performance reviews
- Strategy refresh decks for leadership

Marketing & Sales

- Campaign performance reviews
- Content plans and social metrics
- Lead-gen presentations for webinars or demos

Tactical Best Practices

- **Be Specific in Prompts**: The more context you provide ChatGPT, the closer the result matches your voice and goals.
- **Use ChatGPT to Rewrite Slides**: Paste messy bullets and ask ChatGPT to rewrite in slide-ready format.
- **Create a Template Bank in Canva**: Store frequently-used designs for reports, proposals, and decks.
- **Stick to a Format**: Use the same headings and sections monthly to train your audience.

Common Pitfalls

Too Much Text Per Slide
Use ChatGPT to tighten language: "Rewrite this paragraph as a 5-word bullet list."

Ignoring Visual Hierarchy
Use Canva to adjust layout balance—one idea per slide, consistent font size, and alignment.

Wrong Level of Detail
Ask ChatGPT: "Rewrite for C-level audience" or "Summarize for junior marketers."

Checklist: One-Hour AI Report Workflow

- Gather notes or export data
- Ask ChatGPT for a draft report with summary and insights
- Ask for chart suggestions and slide structure
- Choose Canva template, paste content
- Use Magic Design or Smart Chart tools
- Export as PDF or Google Slides

Conclusion

You no longer need to be a designer or analyst to create high-impact reports and presentations. AI levels the playing field.

With ChatGPT and Canva, you can:

- Save time
- Communicate clearly
- Impress stakeholders

What once took an entire afternoon now takes an hour—with better results.

Coming up next: **Chapter 7: Learning Anything Faster with AI** — we'll show you how to build real skills using smart prompts, adaptive tools, and AI-powered study systems.

Chapter 7

Learning Anything Faster with AI

How to Study Using ChatGPT (Create Tests, Flashcards, etc.)

In a world where the pace of change is constant and the half-life of knowledge keeps shrinking, traditional learning methods often fail to keep up. Whether you're a small business owner brushing up on digital marketing, a consultant staying current with regulations, or a professional learning a new tool—how you learn matters as much as what you learn.

AI—specifically ChatGPT—offers a deeply customizable and responsive way to learn. Unlike static resources or rigid online courses, ChatGPT adapts to your level, format preference, and pace. More importantly, it lets you engage with the material by doing—not just reading.

Let's explore exactly how you can use ChatGPT to turn any topic into an interactive learning system.

The Role of ChatGPT in Self-Directed Learning

AI-powered tutors like ChatGPT eliminate the biggest roadblocks to adult learning:

- Lack of time
- Poor fit between the resource and your background
- Passive consumption (vs. active learning)

With ChatGPT, you can:

- Ask follow-up questions at your level
- Request analogies until something clicks
- Generate your own quizzes, flashcards, or step-by-step guides
- Simulate real-world practice with customized scenarios

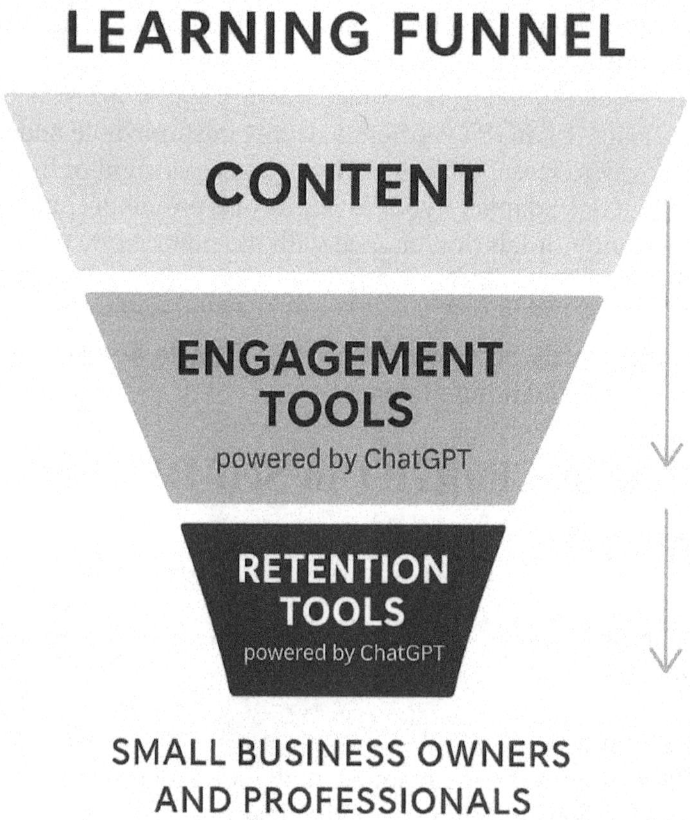

Start With a Learning Goal

You can't learn everything at once. Good AI learning starts with a clear intent. Use this format:

"I want to learn [subject] so I can [real-world goal] by [date]."

Example:

"I want to learn the basics of GDPR so I can ensure our client contracts are compliant by end of Q3."

Now ChatGPT knows how to frame content, test your understanding, and focus examples.

Create Flashcards with ChatGPT

Flashcards are proven memory tools. They force recall (not just recognition), which builds deeper understanding.

Prompt:

"Create 20 flashcards about [topic] formatted as Q&A pairs. Use clear, simple language."

Example:

"Create 20 flashcards about GDPR basics for someone in client services."

ChatGPT outputs:

- Q: What does GDPR stand for?
  A: General Data Protection Regulation
- Q: What's the legal basis for processing data?
  A: Consent, contract, legal obligation, vital interest, public task, or legitimate interest

You can copy this into Quizlet, Anki, or just review manually.

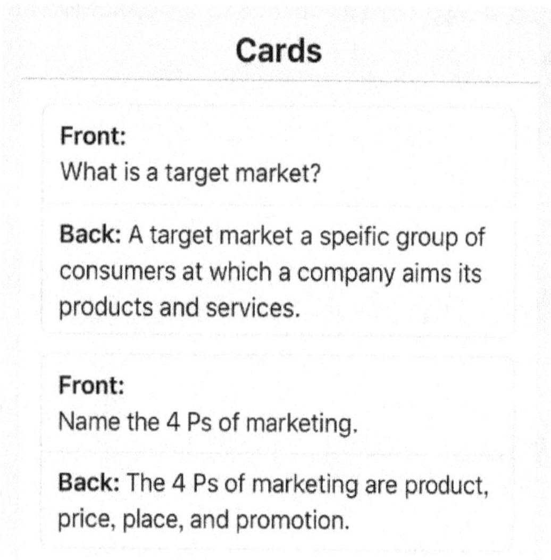

Build Your Own Practice Tests

ChatGPT can simulate quizzes, multiple-choice tests, and even short-answer exams.

Prompt:

"Make a 10-question multiple-choice quiz about [topic]. Include an answer key."

Bonus: Ask ChatGPT to:

- Explain each correct answer
- Add difficulty ratings
- Include a mini case study per question

Business Compliance

Generated by ChatGPT

1. **Which of the following is a key purpose of a compliance program?**
   A) Protecting the company's assets
   B) Ensuring product quality
   C) Promoting innovation
   D) Minimizing regulatory violations
   Answer: D

2. **What is a primary responsibility of a compliance officer?**
   A) Developing new marketing strategies
   B) Overseeing the compliance program
   C) Managing financial investments
   D) Designing employee benefits plans
   Answer: B

Simulate Real Scenarios to Practice Thinking

Learning isn't just about definitions—it's about application.

Prompt:

"Create a realistic scenario where a [role] must make a decision involving [topic]. Ask me what I'd do, then evaluate my response."

Example:

"Create a scenario where an HR manager must decide whether to disclose a data breach under GDPR."

ChatGPT:

- Outlines a situation
- Asks your response
- Provides critique or guidance

This trains judgment, not just memorization.

Transform Notes into Study Guides

Copy-paste your meeting notes, articles, or lecture transcripts into ChatGPT. Then ask:

- "Summarize this into key points"
- "Make this into a checklist"
- "Explain this like I'm a beginner"
- "What are the three most testable concepts here?"

You get tailored, structured summaries without needing to re-read everything.

Schedule AI-Powered Study Sessions

Even 20 minutes a day is enough if it's structured. Use ChatGPT as a pacing tool:

Prompt:

"Help me study [topic] in 15-minute daily sessions over the next 2 weeks. Break it into sessions and include goals."

ChatGPT gives you:

- A 10–14 day curriculum
- Daily mini-goals
- Built-in reviews and tests

It becomes your personal coach.

Common Mistakes to Avoid

- **No Clear Goal**: Vague prompts lead to vague content. Set a purpose first.
- **All Passive Reading**: Force yourself to quiz, rephrase, and explain out loud.
- **Too Much at Once**: Use sessions, not marathons. Review regularly.
- **Ignoring Weak Points**: Ask ChatGPT to test you on past mistakes until they're fixed.

Checklist: Study With ChatGPT

- Define your goal (topic, purpose, timeline)
- Ask for 20 flashcards in Q&A format
- Generate a short quiz to test recall
- Simulate a real scenario in your field
- Paste notes and convert to summaries or checklists
- Build a 2-week daily micro-study plan
- Review and refine your weak areas

Conclusion

AI won't learn for you. But it removes friction from the learning process. ChatGPT turns one-size-fits-none material into bite-sized, personalized, interactive study that matches your time, your goals, and your level.

Coming next: **Personalize Your Learning Plan with Gemini or Claude** — learn how other AI assistants compare and how to use them to go even deeper in your learning path.

Personalize Your Learning Plan with Gemini or Claude

The power of AI in learning lies not just in its ability to teach facts, but in how well it can tailor the learning experience to the individual. While ChatGPT excels at interactive learning, tools like Google's Gemini and Anthropic's Claude bring their own unique strengths to personalizing a self-paced, purpose-driven education. This section explores how to build a tailored learning plan using these assistants—designed for clarity, speed, and retention.

Why Use Gemini or Claude for Learning Personalization?

Both Gemini and Claude are designed to be more narrative, context-sensitive, and long-term oriented than many other AI platforms. That makes them ideal for:

- Long-form learning plans
- Interconnected topics
- Strategy-oriented learners (e.g., consultants, planners, business owners)

They also support deeper memory and context retention—ideal for multi-week learning paths that adapt as you grow.

Step-by-Step: Crafting a Personalized Learning Roadmap

1. Define the Goal

Use a prompt that is explicit about time, role, and purpose.

Prompt:

"I want to learn [topic] over [X weeks] so I can apply it in [role/task]. Please break it down into stages and build a personalized roadmap."

Example:

"I want to learn foundational UX principles over the next 6 weeks so I can apply them to my new product startup."

Claude or Gemini typically responds with a multi-phase breakdown:

- Week 1–2: Core principles
- Week 3–4: Use case scenarios
- Week 5: Tools & processes
- Week 6: Practice project + feedback prompts

2. Adapt to Your Time and Style

Personalization doesn't just mean content—it means format and rhythm.

Prompt:

"I learn best with short articles, diagrams, and examples. Build each week using this style."

Or for verbal learners:

"Summarize this week's topic into a teach-back I can record and repeat aloud."

Claude and Gemini can adapt outputs to:

- Video transcript-style explanations
- Interactive case studies
- Email-style summaries
- One-pager briefings

3. Connect Topics to Your World

Many adult learners disengage when examples feel irrelevant. So get AI to localize your curriculum.

Prompt:

"Use examples relevant to my work as a small business owner in the home services industry."

These systems will adapt:

- Marketing principles → local SEO and booking forms
- Financial learning → cash flow issues in a seasonal business
- Legal learning → contracts with subcontractors

4. Use Checkpoints and Quizzes

Ask Gemini or Claude to build checkpoints that help you measure progress.

Prompt:

"At the end of each week, create a 5-question checkpoint quiz and ask one reflection question."

Gemini, in particular, is strong at:

- Logic-based multiple-choice quizzes
- Prompted journaling
- Self-assessment rubrics

5. Build in Spaced Review

Repetition is key—but only if it's spaced out. You can ask:

Prompt:

"Create a 2-week spaced review schedule to revisit major topics from my UX learning plan. Use active recall."

You'll get:

- Daily or alternate-day reminders
- 2–3 flashback prompts per day
- "One-minute explain it back" exercises

Tactical Best Practices

- Use **Claude** for highly nuanced topics (ethics, language, strategy)
- Use **Gemini** for visual, list-based, or timeline-based learning
- Ask for learning to be delivered in your favorite medium (Google Docs, Markdown, Slide format)
- Use feedback: Tell it what worked and what didn't, and request adjustments
- Repeat goals weekly to reinforce direction

Real-World Example: Learning Business Strategy with Gemini

What Happened

A mid-level operations manager used Gemini to build a personalized 4-week crash course in strategic thinking—something he'd previously only learned by observing execs.

What Went Right

Gemini broke down the topic by function (operations, finance, market), built daily study triggers via Google Calendar, and delivered 3 reflection prompts each Friday.

What We Learned

When learning is tied to job actions (not abstract theory), retention and confidence increase rapidly. AI helped reframe broad strategy into real-world lenses.

Common Pitfalls to Avoid

- **Too Generic Goals**: Vague asks = generic plans.
- **No Format Preference**: Gemini/Claude can shape material how you like—tell them.
- **Skipping Review**: Don't just move on. Revisit and teach back.
- **No Real-Life Anchor**: Tie learning to real business needs.

Checklist: Personalized AI Learning

- Define the end goal and timeline
- Request a weekly roadmap
- Specify your content format preference
- Localize examples to your industry
- Build weekly checkpoints + quizzes
- Schedule review prompts for retention
- Ask for real-world case applications

Conclusion

Personalized learning used to mean paying a private coach. Now, AI tools like Gemini and Claude make it accessible to anyone with a clear goal. The more context you give, the smarter and more usable the content becomes. You stay focused, and your study becomes outcome-oriented, not just fact-based.

Next up: **Create Slide Decks & Infographics Automatically** — because showing what you know matters just as much as learning it.

Create Slide Decks & Infographics Automatically

Creating polished, professional-looking presentations and infographics used to take hours—sometimes days. But with today's AI tools, even non-designers can rapidly turn ideas into impactful visuals without touching PowerPoint templates or hiring freelancers. This section walks you through how to go from a blank page to a compelling presentation or branded infographic in minutes using ChatGPT, Canva AI, and supporting tools like Tome and Gamma.

Why Visual Communication Matters

Whether you're a founder pitching investors, a manager reporting progress, or a consultant delivering insights—how your message looks matters.

Good design builds:

- Trust and professionalism
- Faster comprehension of complex topics
- More persuasive storytelling

But many small businesses and busy professionals skip visual aids because they're time-consuming. That's where AI changes the game.

Slide Decks in Minutes: Using Gamma and Tome

Gamma: AI-Powered Slide Generator

Gamma builds sleek, modern slides from a single prompt. Think "Google Slides meets Notion meets AI." Ideal for startup decks, reports, and client briefings.

Prompt Example:

"Create a 5-slide pitch deck for a new home cleaning subscription startup. Include problem, solution, business model, traction, and CTA."

Gamma auto-generates:

- Slide titles
- Visual layouts
- Section summaries
- Placeholder data visuals

You can then edit, apply themes, and export to PDF or shareable link.

Tome: Narrative-First Presentation Builder

Tome helps you tell a story, not just show slides. It integrates text, visuals, charts, and even AI-generated images in one responsive flow.

Prompt Example:

"Build a presentation explaining how AI can automate HR tasks in a small business. Make it suitable for a 15-minute team talk."

Tome delivers:

- Scroll-based layouts
- Embedded explanations and charts
- Clear narrative arcs (great for training or sales education)

Canva Magic for Infographics & Presentations

Canva AI's "Magic Design" tool is ideal for:

- Infographics
- One-pagers
- Business reports
- Social media carousels

Use Case: Fast-Branded Infographics

Prompt Example (to ChatGPT):

"Summarize the key benefits of remote work into bullet points, data facts, and visual ideas for an infographic."

Take that summary and feed it into Canva:

1. Use the Infographic template category.
2. Paste your copy.
3. Click "Magic Design" to generate layout options.
4. Drag in branded colors, logos, and adjust visuals.

Step-by-Step: From Raw Text to Final Visual

Step 1: Generate Structured Content

Use ChatGPT to break your topic into:

- Title + subtitle
- Sections with headers
- Bullet points
- Data callouts
- Quotes or case studies

Prompt:

"Turn this blog post into a 6-slide presentation outline with bullets, speaker notes, and suggested visuals."

Step 2: Choose the Right Tool

- **Use Gamma** for clean corporate decks
- **Use Tome** for storytelling flows
- **Use Canva** for infographics or quick visual posts

Step 3: Refine and Brand

In Canva:

- Upload your logo, brand colors, and fonts
- Use AI to swap visuals
- Use "Magic Write" for slide text copy improvements

In Gamma or Tome:

- Refine section headers
- Replace placeholders with real stats or screenshots
- Adjust pacing and flow

Tactical Best Practices

- Always give AI a structure to start with: slide count, themes, tone
- Use your existing blog posts or client reports as source material
- Create one master outline and reuse it across formats
- Design for skimmability: large headers, 1 idea per slide, clear visuals
- Add 1–2 real-world stats per slide to anchor trust

Real-World Example: Creating a Marketing Proposal in 30 Minutes

What Happened

A marketing consultant needed a proposal deck for a potential HVAC client.

What Went Right

He used ChatGPT to outline the strategy (SEO, Google Ads, social proof), then Gamma to turn that into slides, added logos and charts, and delivered a 6-slide deck in under 30 minutes.

What We Learned

AI removes design friction. The expert's insight stayed the focus—presentation just became frictionless.

Common Pitfalls

- **Asking for too much at once**: Break requests into 3–6 slide chunks
- **Skipping content checks**: Review all AI text before presenting
- **Too much decoration**: Stick to clean, visual, branded
- **Forgetting calls to action**: Always end decks with a "next step"

Checklist: AI-Driven Visual Content Creation

- Outline your key message in 4–6 slides or blocks
- Use ChatGPT to structure content
- Choose Gamma, Tome, or Canva based on format
- Apply your brand kit or colors
- Review visuals for clarity, accuracy, and tone
- Export to PDF, deck, or web format

Conclusion

Creating presentations and infographics isn't a design problem anymore—it's a thinking problem. AI tools like Gamma, Tome, and Canva Magic remove the complexity and help you communicate faster and smarter. Your ideas still drive the story—AI just helps you package them like a pro.

Next up: **Learn Languages, Math, History & More via AI Tutors** — discover how to turn AI into your personal classroom, coach, and curriculum builder.

Learn Languages, Math, History & More via AI Tutors

For small business owners, entrepreneurs, and consultants, time is the most precious resource. Learning something new—whether a language to expand into new markets, math to better understand financials, or history to make better strategic decisions—often falls by the wayside. AI tutors are beginning to change that, putting on-demand, personalized education within reach of any professional, at any level, in any location.

AI tutoring isn't a distant dream or a Silicon Valley-only tool. These systems are already reshaping how adults upskill, how teams build domain expertise, and how learning fits into even the busiest schedules. This chapter dives into how AI-powered tutors work, why they're so effective, and what practical ways business leaders can use them to grow professionally and competitively.

The Shift From Static Learning to Dynamic Mentorship

Traditional learning platforms offer pre-packaged content: a video here, a multiple-choice quiz there. They assume a passive learner and provide a one-size-fits-all approach. AI tutors invert that model. Instead of delivering the same material to everyone, they respond to the user's inputs, questions, and performance in real-time.

AI tutors use natural language processing to understand how you ask questions, machine learning to evaluate how quickly you grasp concepts, and reinforcement learning to adapt their teaching strategies over time. Think of them less like apps and more like highly trained coaches who never get tired, distracted, or judgmental.

Key Use Cases for Professionals

Whether you're trying to brush up on high school algebra or learn conversational French for an expansion into Quebec, the applications are immediate:

- **Languages**: AI tutors offer real-time conversation practice, pronunciation correction, grammar coaching, and even cultural context tips.
- **Math & Data Skills**: From understanding interest rates to learning spreadsheet logic or basic statistics, AI tutors break down concepts step-by-step.
- **History & Strategic Thinking**: By walking through historical case studies or major geopolitical events, AI tutors help contextualize decision-making with global awareness.
- **Certifications & Exams**: Studying for PMP, CPA, or even cybersecurity certifications? AI tutors tailor study plans and simulate test conditions based on your performance.

Tactical Best Practices

- **Set a Consistent Schedule**: Learning thrives on habit. Use 20-minute daily blocks rather than binge sessions.
- **Define a Learning Outcome**: Don't "learn Spanish." Learn "how to pitch our product to a Spanish-speaking customer."
- **Leverage Multimodal Input**: Use text, voice, and even image inputs (where supported) to create a richer interaction.
- **Ask Dumb Questions**: AI doesn't judge. Use it to clarify things you might hesitate to ask a human tutor.
- **Tie Learning to Business Needs**: Apply concepts in your business immediately. Learn percentages by reviewing P&L, or practice French by translating your own emails.

Common Pitfalls or Mistakes

- **Overreliance on Passive Use**: Watching AI-generated summaries or lessons without engaging doesn't result in lasting knowledge.
- **No Feedback Loop**: Without applying knowledge or asking follow-up questions, the learning stalls.
- **Trying to Learn Everything**: Spreading too thin makes retention difficult. Stick to one goal per learning sprint.
- **Using Free Tools Without Strategy**: Many free AI tutors lack customization. Know what you're sacrificing when you opt for them.

Real-World Example

What Happened

A small marketing firm in Austin wanted to expand services into Latin America. The founder, fluent only in English, needed basic Spanish comprehension and business etiquette knowledge—fast. Instead of enrolling in a six-month class, he used an AI language tutor every morning during his commute, asking it to simulate business meetings and correct his responses.

What Went Right

Because the AI tutor adapted to his level, he quickly skipped beginner lessons and honed in on terminology related to sales, contracts, and cultural nuance. After eight weeks, he could participate in client meetings with a local translator, often understanding 70–80% of the conversation unaided.

What We Learn From It

The key wasn't the tool, but the focus. By setting a business outcome and treating the AI like a daily accountability partner, the founder accelerated learning dramatically without overloading his schedule.

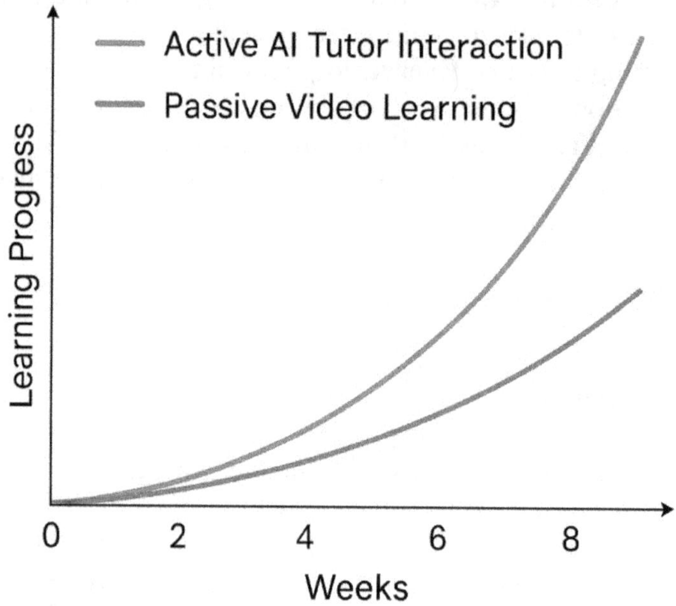

When AI Tutors Work Best

- **Skill Gaps Are Defined**: AI tutors need to know what you want. They excel when the learning objective is clear.
- **Time Is Limited**: They adapt to 10-minute or 30-minute windows with equal efficiency.
- **Confidence Needs Boosting**: For those embarrassed by "elementary" questions, AI is a safe training ground.
- **Human Tutoring Isn't Feasible**: Whether due to cost, location, or timing, AI provides scalable alternatives.

Checklist-Style Action Steps

1. **Identify the Skill You Need**: Choose a single, high-value learning goal.
2. **Pick a Trusted AI Tutor Platform**: Look for options that offer real-time feedback and memory of past interactions.
3. **Schedule Time Daily**: Use calendar holds to create a consistent learning habit.
4. **Use Contextual Prompts**: Frame your learning inside your actual work (e.g., "Explain EBITDA like I'm reviewing a client's financials").
5. **Measure Progress Weekly**: Keep a simple log of what you've learned, applied, and what's next.
6. **Apply in the Real World**: Integrate new knowledge directly into your tasks, calls, or planning sessions.
7. **Adjust as Needed**: Let the AI know when you're stuck, bored, or ready for more.

7-DAY AI TUTORING SCHEDULE

for a business owner learning basic accounting terms

DAY	TOPIC
Monday	Assets and Liabilities
Tuesday	Revenue and Expenses
Wednesday	Equity
Thursday	Accounts Receivable and Payable
Friday	Income Statement
Saturday	Balance Sheet
Sunday	Cash Flow

Ethical & Practical Limits

AI tutors aren't substitutes for expertise in complex, regulated fields. They can teach you how to calculate ROI, but not how to interpret a legal document in another language. They can drill math formulas, but not replace a CPA. Recognize where human expertise is essential, and where AI can bridge the confidence gap.

Also, ensure privacy settings are understood. Some platforms retain interactions. If discussing business-sensitive topics, check the data handling policies.

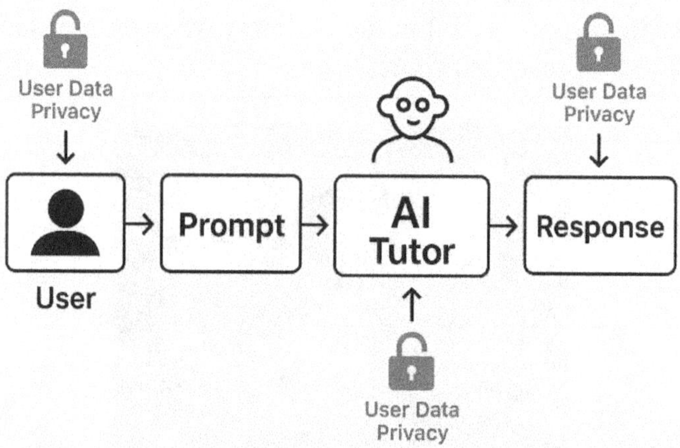

Conclusion

AI tutors are transforming how professionals learn—not by replacing schools or mentors, but by making personalized, context-driven education scalable. For SMB leaders, consultants, and founders, this means upskilling can happen in between client calls, during flights, or over lunch. The key is to tie learning directly to your business priorities and let AI handle the repetition, the feedback, and the schedule.

Next Steps

In the next section, we'll look at how AI doesn't just teach but helps you **track your learning, goals, and time** with smart planners and workflow tools. As you grow your capabilities, you'll need a system to manage and measure that progress. Let's explore how AI-powered planning tools do exactly that—without adding more to your plate.

Tracking Progress & Goals with AI-Powered Planners

For any business leader, consultant, or founder trying to juggle strategy, operations, growth, and personal development, staying organized can feel like trying to hold water in your hands. Traditional planning tools—calendars, notebooks, even spreadsheets—weren't built to think *with* you. They help track what you tell them, but they don't notice when you drift, suggest better priorities, or help you adapt when circumstances change. That's where AI-powered planning tools are breaking new ground.

These systems are more than just "to-do" apps with smart interfaces. They combine task tracking, calendar syncing, goal alignment, and real-time analysis of your habits and progress. Think of them as executive assistants that don't just manage your time, but help optimize your *outcomes*. When used effectively, AI planners can shift the way business leaders execute priorities—not just by recording what needs to be done, but by actively participating in making sure it gets done.

Why AI Planning Tools Are Game-Changers

AI planners differ from digital tools like Google Calendar or Trello in a few powerful ways:

- **They learn your patterns**: After a few weeks of use, an AI planner can detect when you're most productive, when you're most likely to miss deadlines, and when meetings tend to run long.

- **They align tasks to outcomes**: Rather than isolated tasks, AI planners can help tie your daily to-dos to broader OKRs (Objectives and Key Results), business KPIs, or learning goals.
- **They adjust dynamically**: Get pulled into an emergency? The AI can reflow your schedule automatically to preserve your high-priority goals.
- **They highlight gaps**: If you're not making time for learning, or neglecting team check-ins, they notice—and suggest corrections.

For busy professionals, the value isn't just convenience—it's strategic. These tools help protect your time, realign your efforts, and make your workdays reflect your real priorities.

Real Use Cases for Founders

Let's bring this down to earth. Here are real-world scenarios where AI planners deliver measurable results:

- **Quarterly Goal Tracking**: A consultant defines three strategic initiatives for Q3. The AI planner breaks them into weekly milestones, allocates time on the calendar, and nudges progress updates every Friday.
- **Time Use Audits**: An agency founder uses AI to analyze two weeks of calendar data. It reveals 36% of time is spent on reactive work—client support, unplanned calls. She adjusts her calendar to preserve two focus blocks daily.
- **Team Coordination**: A growing startup uses AI-planning to assign cross-functional tasks. When one team slips, the planner suggests which dependencies are at risk and prompts updates.
- **Health and Burnout Detection**: The planner flags signs of overload (late work, skipped breaks, weekend task catch-ups) and recommends rebalancing. This kind of insight can reduce burnout and turnover.

Tactical Best Practices

- **Start With One Domain**: Don't try to plan your whole life. Start with business goals, then expand.
- **Define Outcomes First**: Let the planner know the "why" behind each task. That context matters.
- **Use It Daily**: Like a fitness tracker, the more you use it, the smarter and more helpful it becomes.
- **Review Weekly**: AI isn't magic. You still need to step back weekly to accept/reject its suggestions.
- **Integrate With Existing Tools**: The best AI planners work with Gmail, Outlook, Slack, and others.

Common Pitfalls or Mistakes

- **Over-Automation**: Letting AI re-prioritize everything can cause confusion or misalignment with human goals.
- **Neglecting Review**: AI suggestions aren't always right. Use judgment.
- **Lack of Clarity in Goals**: Vague inputs like "grow the business" don't help AI know what to schedule or how to track.
- **Ignoring Personal Limits**: Just because AI says you can do more doesn't mean you should. Protect recovery time.

Real-World Example

What Happened

A regional real estate firm adopted an AI planner to help its five agents and one operations manager stay aligned. Each agent had individual revenue goals, marketing responsibilities, and community events to attend. Before AI planning, coordination was ad hoc, and end-of-month scrambles were routine.

What Went Right

By feeding each person's quarterly targets into the planner and syncing all team calendars, the AI could forecast when people were overbooked or under-tasked. It helped redistribute effort, avoid burnout, and ensure follow-through on marketing initiatives. Within one quarter, total lead generation rose by 27% and employee stress (self-reported) dropped by half.

What We Learn From It

AI planners are most powerful when used to *coordinate effort toward shared goals*. They're not just personal assistants—they become operational infrastructure for agile, distributed teams.

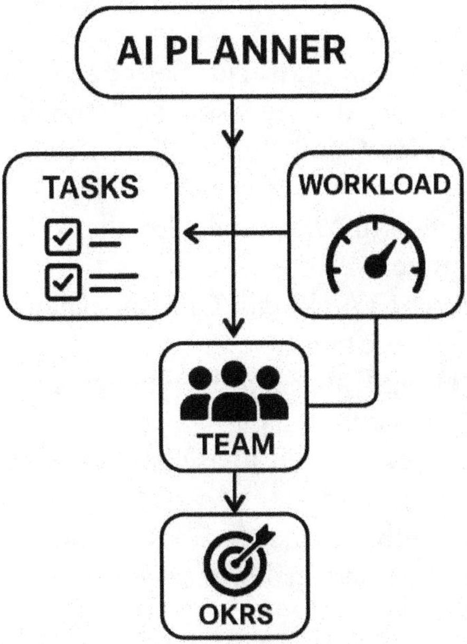

ADJUSTING TEAM TASKS
BASED ON WORKLOAD
AND SHARED OKRS

How AI Tracks Progress Effectively

The value isn't just in planning—it's in the feedback loop. Here's how AI helps track and improve over time:

- **Milestone Recognition**: It knows when you complete a major step and automatically logs progress.
- **Predictive Warnings**: Missed small deadlines? The AI can alert you if a big milestone is at risk.
- **Goal Drift Detection**: If you're spending too much time on low-impact tasks, it flags the imbalance.
- **Learning Loop**: AI learns from how you shift tasks, defer actions, or complete work faster/slower than planned.

Checklist-Style Action Steps

1. **Choose a Planner Platform**: Select a tool with proven AI capability, calendar integration, and outcome tracking.
2. **Define 1–3 Key Goals**: Input what success looks like in 90 days.
3. **Break Goals into Milestones**: Let the AI help distribute the steps over time.
4. **Input Current Workload**: Give the planner access to your calendar and task tools.
5. **Start Tracking Daily**: Let the planner suggest priorities, start times, and durations.
6. **Evaluate Weekly**: Adjust based on progress, planner insights, and new data.
7. **Expand Carefully**: Once business planning is humming, consider adding personal or team layers.

When It Works Best

- **During Strategic Pivots**: When your goals change, the planner helps rewire priorities.
- **Across Distributed Teams**: AI planners unify remote teams around visible, trackable outcomes.
- **For High-Achieving Leaders**: If you're always at 100% capacity, a smart planner keeps you honest about bandwidth.
- **During Learning Sprints**: AI can make sure your learning stays on track amidst daily chaos.

Ethical Considerations & Privacy

Most AI planners rely on data access to deliver insights. That can include:

- Calendar invites and meeting titles
- Email metadata
- Task descriptions
- Time spent in various apps

Before adopting one, check:

- **Data Retention Policies**: How long does the system store your data?
- **Control Over Deletion**: Can you wipe history completely?
- **Data Use**: Are your patterns being used to train public models?
- **Vendor Trustworthiness**: Choose platforms with third-party audits and enterprise customers.

The Role of Human Oversight

Even the smartest AI planner needs a human in the loop. It can prioritize, suggest, warn—but it can't know your gut feeling, market pulse, or evolving strategy. Use these tools to *augment* your decision-making, not replace it.

Your role is to:

- Accept or reject re-prioritizations
- Feed in updated goals and blockers
- Periodically recalibrate strategy

That's the magic: AI handles the complexity. You stay focused on leadership.

Conclusion

AI-powered planners are becoming the executive function support system that time-strapped professionals never had. For founders, consultants, and team leaders alike, they offer more than productivity—they offer *clarity*. Clear goals, clear signals, and clear next steps. In an age where distraction is the default, that clarity is a superpower.

Next Steps

In the next chapter, we turn from productivity to protection. As these powerful tools become embedded in our daily workflows, the risks around data privacy, ethical use, and overdependence become very real. In **Chapter 8: Staying Safe & Ethical**, we'll dive into how to harness AI responsibly, protect your team's privacy, and build trust into your AI stack from day one.

Chapter 8

Staying Safe & Ethical

What Data AI Collects (and How to Protect Yourself)

Every time you use an AI system—whether it's generating a business plan, analyzing sales data, or helping you write a customer response—you're creating a digital fingerprint. That fingerprint is made up of more than just words or clicks; it includes patterns, preferences, metadata, and behavioral traits. And the companies behind these tools, unless explicitly told otherwise, may retain, reuse, or analyze that data for their own purposes.

For founders, consultants, and business owners, the implications aren't just personal. Your data may include client names, sales forecasts, internal strategy, or proprietary methods. If that information is not handled securely, you're not just risking your own privacy—you're putting your team, clients, and company at risk.

This chapter breaks down what data AI systems actually collect, how it's used, and most critically, how to protect your business against unintended exposure or misuse.

The Hidden Layers of AI Data Collection

AI tools collect far more than just the text you type or the image you upload. Here's a breakdown of what gets captured:

1. Direct Input Data

This includes everything you actively give the tool:

- Prompts and queries
- Uploaded documents or images
- Code snippets or audio files

2. Metadata

Metadata is data about your data. It includes:

- Timestamps
- File names and extensions
- Language or location settings
- Device type and browser fingerprint

3. Interaction Data

AI systems track how you use them:

- Session duration and click paths
- Revisions, deletions, and re-prompts
- Frequency and time of use
- Response ratings (thumbs up/down)

4. Behavioral and Usage Patterns

Advanced models build profiles over time:

- Topics of interest or expertise
- Communication tone or style
- Preferred formats and structures
- Risk thresholds (e.g., how cautious or bold your responses are)

How That Data Is Used (With and Without Consent)

Different AI platforms have different data policies, but here's how your data is typically used:

- **To Improve the Model**: Some providers use your inputs to train future versions of the model.

- **To Personalize Responses**: Memory-enabled systems store your preferences and use history.
- **To Monitor Abuse or Harm**: AI companies may review usage for compliance or safety.
- **To Monetize Insights**: Anonymized data might be used to spot trends or develop new features.

The problem? Not all providers are clear about where they draw the line between personalization and surveillance. And many SMB users never read the fine print.

Real-World Example

What Happened

A small legal consultancy used an AI writing assistant to help draft client contracts. The assistant learned the firm's preferred clauses and writing tone over time. Months later, a paralegal noticed that the AI suggested a clause originally written for another client—raising alarms about cross-case data exposure.

What Went Wrong

The firm had opted into a "beta testing" program that allowed the provider to retain and reuse prompts to improve performance. That meant confidential legal templates were potentially used as training data.

What We Learn From It

Even anonymized or repurposed use of data can create exposure. If your AI provider doesn't clearly separate your business data from its training data, you may be bleeding IP without knowing it.

Tactical Best Practices

- **Read the Data Policy, Not Just the Features**: Before onboarding any AI tool, locate and review its privacy and retention documentation.
- **Use Business vs. Consumer Plans**: Enterprise or business-tier accounts typically come with stricter data separation.
- **Turn Off Data Sharing**: Most platforms have a toggle in settings. Make sure you opt out where possible.
- **Segment Confidential Work**: Don't draft legal, HR, or financial content in free or generic AI tools.
- **Audit Your Inputs**: If you wouldn't post it publicly, don't paste it into a system you don't fully control.

Common Pitfalls or Mistakes

- **Assuming Anonymization Equals Safety**: Metadata can still reveal authorship or context.
- **Mixing Personal and Work Accounts**: This creates leakage between environments, especially when synced with cloud storage.
- **Ignoring Consent Checkboxes**: Beta programs, product surveys, and "improve quality" toggles often involve deeper data collection.
- **Relying on Word-of-Mouth Trust**: Just because a platform is popular doesn't mean it's secure.

Checklist-Style Protection Plan

1. **Identify Tools in Use**: List every AI tool you or your team use—even trial versions.
2. **Map Input Types**: What kind of data is being shared? (e.g., names, financials, strategy notes)
3. **Review Terms of Service**: Focus on sections titled "Data Use," "Retention," or "Training."

4. **Disable Memory or History Where Possible**: Especially if you're working with sensitive content.
5. **Use Dummy Data for Testing**: Never use real client or company data when evaluating a new tool.
6. **Switch to Private Environments**: Use local or on-prem tools when confidentiality is essential.
7. **Train Staff on Safe Prompting**: Everyone should know what *not* to share with AI.

AI Data Risks by Industry

Different sectors face different exposure levels:

- **Legal**: Client names, contract language, privileged communications
- **Finance**: Account data, projections, internal audits
- **Healthcare**: PHI, diagnosis notes, lab results
- **Marketing**: Customer personas, campaign copy, brand strategy
- **Education**: Student records, grading rubrics, unpublished research

INDUSTRY	AI DATA RISK EXPOSURE	RECOMMENDED SAFEGUARDS
Healthcare	HIGH	Strict data anonymization & access controls
Legal	HIGH	Client-attorney privilege maintained
Finance	MEDIUM	Encryption & AI audit trrails
Marketing	MEDIUM	Limit use of third-party data
Government	HIGH	Strict regulations public transpar-
Technology	LOW	Employee training & secure development

The Myth of “Safe” Prompts

Even generic prompts like "Write a sales pitch for my latest product" can leak strategy. Why?

- **Product details may be proprietary**
- **Language reveals positioning**
- **Style and tone can indicate brand identity**

Unless you're working in a closed, isolated environment, assume that *anything* typed could theoretically be stored or reviewed. Operate with the same discretion you would in a recorded call.

How to Vet an AI Vendor

Before integrating AI into any operational workflow, ask vendors:

- Does your tool store or reuse my prompts?
- Can I opt out of training data collection?
- Where is my data physically stored?
- Who can access it (human reviewers, subcontractors, etc.)?
- What certifications or audits does your platform undergo?

Good vendors will answer directly and in plain English. If answers are vague or buried in legalese, consider it a red flag.

Data Minimization as a Strategy

The best way to reduce risk is to reduce exposure. A few guiding principles:

- **Only input what’s needed**: Don’t give the AI your full plan—just the component you need help with.
- **Strip identifiers**: Remove names, emails, account numbers, or IP.

- **Use placeholders**: e.g., "{Client_Name}" instead of real names.
- **Work offline first**: Draft sensitive content locally, then use AI only for formatting or summary help.

Conclusion

AI systems are powerful allies—but they're also data sponges. And the more they know about you, your business, and your clients, the more risk they carry if mishandled. Treat AI like you would a new hire with access to sensitive documents: trust is earned, oversight is constant, and data access is given on a strict need-to-know basis.

Next Steps

In the next section, we'll break down the *exact* privacy settings to change across popular AI platforms—and why most of them are hidden by default. In **Privacy Settings You Should Change Immediately**, you'll learn how to lock down your tools without compromising performance.

Privacy Settings You Should Change Immediately

After understanding the types of data AI platforms collect, the next critical step is control. Many privacy risks tied to AI usage are not caused by hackers or malware—they stem from default settings, unchecked permissions, and vague consent language buried deep in service agreements. Fortunately, most of these can be managed. You don't need to become a cybersecurity expert to dramatically reduce your exposure—you just need to know which switches to flip.

This chapter walks you through the most critical privacy settings to change across AI platforms, productivity tools, browsers, and cloud environments. These are settings that affect real businesses, real users, and real consequences.

Why Privacy Settings Matter More Than Ever

AI systems are not static tools—they are often cloud-connected, continuously learning, and highly integrated with other platforms. That means small privacy oversights can compound quickly. For example:

- A document uploaded to an AI assistant may be stored in a training environment.
- A shared calendar synced with an AI scheduler could leak meeting topics.
- An AI chatbot with memory turned on might retain private client names or pricing details.

In many cases, the tool isn't doing anything wrong per its terms of service—it's doing exactly what was enabled by default. Your job is to disable what you don't want.

High-Risk Defaults to Watch Out For

1. **Memory or History Enabled by Default**
2. **Prompt Sharing for Model Improvement**
3. **Cross-App Data Sharing (e.g., Gmail + Docs + Chat)**
4. **Auto-Sync with Cloud Drives or Calendars**
5. **Open Access Permissions ("Anyone with the link can view")**

These defaults aren't inherently malicious, but they are designed to maximize performance, not confidentiality. It's your responsibility to realign them for business safety.

Real-World Example

What Happened

A freelance consultant used a free AI summarizer tool to analyze PDF proposals from various clients. The platform had a "community enhancement" toggle enabled by default. Several weeks later, a different user saw phrasing from that consultant's private document auto-populate in a generated summary.

What Went Wrong

The tool stored user inputs and shared anonymized versions to improve its output. The consultant didn't realize that uploading sensitive client files into this environment made their content part of the shared model.

What We Learn From It

If you're uploading anything you wouldn't post on your website, change the settings *first*. Default settings often lean toward maximum data intake. Adjust before you engage.

Critical AI Privacy Settings (Platform-Specific Guidance)

ChatGPT (and Similar Tools)

- **Memory**: Turn off memory to prevent the system from storing prior chats.
- **Chat History & Training**: Disable "Improve model performance" or similar settings.
- **Custom Instructions**: Avoid adding confidential or personally identifying details.
- **Download & Delete Data**: Use the account settings to request your data and purge stored logs.

Microsoft Copilot / 365 AI

- **Admin Controls**: Set organization-wide rules on data retention and visibility.
- **Contextual Access**: Turn off default auto-integration with OneDrive or Outlook unless explicitly needed.
- **Data Sharing to Microsoft**: Review enterprise settings on telemetry and diagnostic feedback.

Google Workspace AI Tools (Docs, Gemini, etc.)

- **AI Suggestions Logging**: Turn off learning from your documents unless you manage a closed enterprise instance.
- **Shared Drive Settings**: Restrict AI access to only essential folders.
- **Cross-Service Integration**: Disable syncing between Gmail, Chat, and Docs where sensitive content overlaps.

Browser-Based AI Extensions

- **Permissions**: Use browser tools to block clipboard access and file downloads.
- **Incognito Mode Defaults**: Many extensions still run in incognito unless explicitly disabled.
- **Script Blocking**: Use tools like uBlock or NoScript to manage tracking scripts from AI tool integrations.

Third-Party Scheduling & Planner AI Tools

- **Calendar Metadata**: Hide meeting titles, attendees, and notes by default.
- **Email Parsing**: Disable automatic scanning of inbox content unless fully encrypted.
- **Data Retention**: Set auto-delete cycles for past meeting data and summaries.

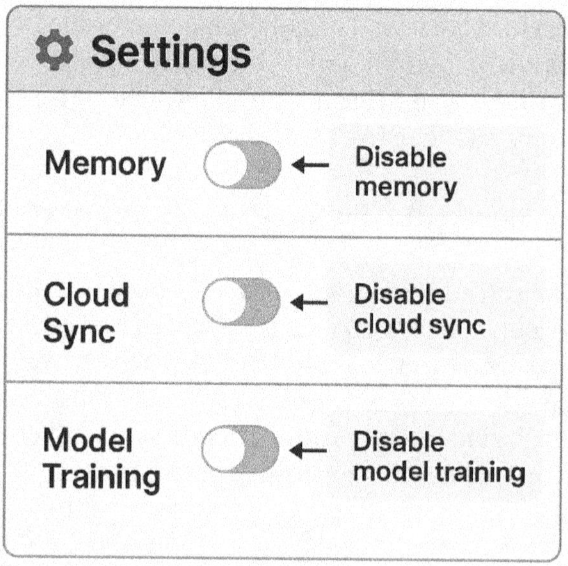

Tactical Best Practices

- **Set Up First Use Carefully**: Don't click "Next" blindly. Assume every toggle is a data collector until proven otherwise.
- **Use Separate Accounts**: Separate personal, client, and internal usage to reduce crossover.
- **Monitor for Policy Updates**: Privacy settings often reset after major updates—re-check quarterly.
- **Request an Audit Trail**: For team use, check if the tool logs who accessed what and when.
- **Set Up Alerts**: Use DLP (Data Loss Prevention) tools or simple alerts for unauthorized access.

Common Mistakes to Avoid

- **Trusting Default Labels**: "Private" doesn't always mean encrypted. "Memory off" may still log usage data.
- **Skipping the Admin Panel**: Especially for business accounts, key settings are only available to account admins.
- **Assuming GDPR/CCPA Means Secure**: These laws restrict data use *after* collection—they don't stop the tool from storing it.
- **Relying Solely on App Permissions**: You also need browser, OS, and network-level controls.

Checklist: Privacy Lockdown for Business AI Use

1. **Audit All AI Tools** in your business ecosystem.
2. **Map Default Settings** for each (memory, sync, retention, sharing).
3. **Disable Data Sharing and Model Training** where applicable.
4. **Enforce Account Segmentation** by role or use case.

5. **Use Encrypted Channels** for all uploads and exports.
6. **Regularly Review Access Logs and Permissions**.
7. **Set an Internal Policy**: Document what should *never* be shared with external AI tools.

Privacy Settings in Mobile AI Apps

AI tools on phones pose special risks:

- **Microphone Access**: Disable unless actively using voice commands.
- **Photo & File Access**: Restrict to only selected folders.
- **Location Data**: Prevent tools from tagging inputs with GPS unless needed for function.
- **Push Notification Content**: Ensure that sensitive data isn't sent in previews.

Integrating AI Without Inviting Risk

Use these tips to stay agile without overexposing:

- Use local or self-hosted models when possible.
- Segment data by use case: marketing content can be shared, client contracts should not.
- Work in layers: Even if one layer leaks, another (like redaction or sandboxing) can protect the whole.

Questions to Ask Before Enabling a New Feature

- Does this increase the model's memory of our work?
- Will this data be visible to anyone outside our org?
- Can this setting be turned off later—or will data already be retained?
- What's the worst-case scenario if this data leaked tomorrow?

These questions aren't meant to scare but to sharpen your decisions.

Conclusion

AI platforms don't announce when they're collecting too much. That's your job. The right privacy settings don't slow down progress—they accelerate it by giving you confidence, compliance, and control. When you know your tools are locked down, you can focus on what matters: serving clients, growing your business, and applying AI where it makes a difference.

Next Steps

Up next, we turn to the darker side of AI: manipulation and fraud. In **Spotting Deepfakes, Fake Reviews, and AI Scams**, you'll learn how to recognize digital deception before it damages your reputation or wallet.

Spotting Deepfakes, Fake Reviews, and AI Scams

The rise of generative AI has unlocked massive productivity and innovation—but it has also opened the floodgates to a new generation of digital deception. From deepfakes that mimic real voices and faces, to AI-generated product reviews and phishing scams indistinguishable from legitimate communication, today's business leaders need more than firewalls. They need vigilance, discernment, and specific strategies to tell real from fake.

For founders, consultants, and operational leaders, falling for an AI-powered scam doesn't just risk financial loss—it can damage brand credibility, mislead customers, and even result in legal exposure. This chapter breaks down how to spot synthetic deception, respond to it, and train your team to do the same.

Understanding the Threat Landscape

AI-powered deception tools are improving rapidly and are now:

- **Cheap to deploy**: Open-source tools and marketplaces make it easy for bad actors to scale scams.
- **Highly convincing**: Voice cloning, video deepfakes, and realistic text blur the line between fake and authentic.
- **Hard to trace**: Many scams originate outside jurisdictional boundaries and use anonymizing tools.

Types of AI-Driven Deception

1. Deepfakes (Video & Audio)

Deepfakes use machine learning to mimic faces, voices, and mannerisms. They've been used to impersonate CEOs, authorize wire transfers, or make public statements that were never actually spoken.

What to watch for:

- Inconsistent lighting or blinking in videos
- Lip-sync issues
- Unusual pauses or vocal tone shifts

2. Fake Reviews & Testimonials

AI can generate large volumes of product reviews, service testimonials, or social proof content that looks human but is entirely synthetic. These flood marketplaces, skew reputation scores, and manipulate buyer decisions.

What to watch for:

- Overly generic praise ("Great service! Highly recommend!")
- Identical phrasing across multiple listings
- Reviewer accounts with no history

3. AI Phishing & Social Engineering

AI tools can write eerily convincing emails, texts, and even voicemails. They adapt tone, reference real data, and use persuasion tactics lifted from real communication patterns.

What to watch for:

- Time-sensitive language: "Immediate action required"
- Personalization that seems accurate but unfamiliar
- Emails from internal-looking domains that are slightly off (e.g., `yourfirm.co` instead of `yourfirm.com`)

4. Synthetic Influencers & Brand Impersonators

Fake personas, complete with AI-generated faces and bios, can be used to launch influencer-style marketing campaigns, impersonate support agents, or infiltrate professional networks.

What to watch for:

- Unusual engagement patterns (e.g., thousands of likes but no real replies)
- No record of offline presence (events, interviews, etc.)
- Profile photos that trigger reverse image search results from AI art platforms

Real-World Example

What Happened

A CFO at a UK energy firm received a video call from what appeared to be the CEO, urgently requesting approval of a high-value transfer to a new vendor. The video matched the CEO's face and voice. The CFO complied—only to discover later that it was a deepfake.

What Went Wrong

The fraudsters had scraped publicly available videos, used AI to clone the CEO's likeness, and timed the request during a known travel window. There was no verification process in place for urgent approvals.

What We Learn From It

Even seasoned professionals can be fooled when trust is visually or vocally manipulated. Verification protocols must outpace synthetic capabilities.

Tactical Best Practices

- **Use Two-Step Verification for All High-Risk Requests**: Especially for payments, contracts, and sensitive approvals.
- **Train Staff to Identify Red Flags**: Provide examples of common phrases and tactics used in AI-generated phishing.
- **Establish Internal Verification Codes or Phrases**: Human-authenticated phrases can outwit AI imitators.
- **Log and Report Suspicious Interactions**: Use centralized tools to report and analyze patterns.
- **Disable Auto-Play for Incoming Video Calls**: Especially in finance, HR, or legal teams.

Common Pitfalls or Mistakes

- **Assuming AI Scams Only Target Large Enterprises**: SMBs are easier marks with less red tape.
- **Relying on Visual Verification Alone**: Deepfakes are built to exploit this trust mechanism.
- **Ignoring Non-Verbal Clues**: Look for hesitation, silence gaps, or abnormal timing in requests.
- **Failing to Review Public Exposure**: Your own leadership videos, bios, and media appearances can be weaponized.

Checklist: Deepfake & Scam Defense Readiness

1. **Map Your Exposure**: What public content could be used to impersonate your team?
2. **Review Critical Workflows**: Where could a fake voice or email insert itself?
3. **Establish Verification Protocols**: No sensitive task should be approved on voice or video alone.
4. **Train Teams Quarterly**: Update phishing and impersonation awareness with live examples.
5. **Use External Monitoring**: Brand protection tools can flag misuse or impersonation attempts online.
6. **Respond Fast**: If a scam is attempted, inform vendors, clients, and internal stakeholders immediately.

AI-Generated Fake Reviews: How to Spot and Respond

- **Look for Behavioral Clustering**: Spikes in 5-star reviews after a negative incident are often artificial.
- **Use Verified Buyer Filters**: These are harder for bots to spoof.
- **Flag and Report Suspicious Content**: Platforms respond faster when reported by affected businesses.
- **Educate Customers**: Transparency about how you validate reviews builds trust.

Signs of AI-Generated Copy in Communications

AI-generated messages often exhibit:

- Polished but generic tone
- Lack of specific context or incorrect references
- Repetition of phrases in unnatural ways
- Misspellings that suggest phonetic confusion (e.g., "site" for "sight")

Train your staff to slow down when they see emails or messages that feel "off," even if superficially professional.

Preventative Tech You Can Deploy

- **Voice Authentication Systems**: Not just passwords—voiceprint matching can flag fraud.
- **Watermarking Content**: Use invisible digital marks on official videos and public statements.
- **Email Authentication Protocols**: Set up SPF, DKIM, and DMARC to prevent spoofing.
- **Content Authenticity Verification**: Use services that verify media origin (e.g., Adobe Content Credentials).

The Human Firewall Still Matters Most

Technology helps—but trained people are your frontline defense. In SMBs, that means every employee is a vector or a shield. Building a culture of curiosity, skepticism, and accountability is more effective than any software suite.

Encourage staff to:

- Confirm strange requests—even from senior leaders
- Log what seems "weird," not just what's obviously wrong
- Stay updated on the latest scam formats (internal newsletters, security briefings)

Conclusion

AI-enabled deception isn't coming—it's already here. The same tools that automate content and productivity are being turned toward fraud at scale. But with informed teams, smart protocols, and the right combination of technology and awareness, businesses can stay not just one step ahead—but several.

Next Steps

In the next section, we'll pivot from detection to discernment. In **8.4 Responsible AI Use: Don't Automate Everything**, we'll explore where *not* to use AI, and why some business decisions still demand a human voice, a human pause, and a human conscience.

Responsible AI Use: Don't Automate Everything

There is a quiet but dangerous assumption taking root in business circles: if AI can do it, it should. After all, automation promises speed, scale, and reduced overhead. But just because AI *can* automate something doesn't mean it should replace human judgment, empathy, or oversight. Responsible AI use means making careful, case-by-case decisions about where human involvement remains not only helpful, but essential.

This chapter offers a reality check for founders, consultants, and growing teams using AI in operations, marketing, customer service, HR, and beyond. If you want your business to remain credible, trustworthy, and legally compliant, knowing where *not* to automate is just as important as knowing what to automate.

Why Over-Automation Creates Risk

Every automation decision carries trade-offs:

- **Speed vs. Context**: AI can respond instantly, but may miss cultural nuance, policy changes, or interpersonal cues.
- **Efficiency vs. Ethics**: Streamlining decisions—especially in hiring, pricing, or customer support—can cause harm if ethical considerations are removed.
- **Scale vs. Trust**: Customers and employees can feel dehumanized when they sense they're dealing with a machine.

Let's break these trade-offs down across real business functions.

Customer-Facing Automation: Where to Draw the Line

What AI Can Do Well

- Triage support tickets
- Provide basic product info
- Generate draft responses for review
- Surface common questions and resources

Where Humans Still Matter

- Handling complaints and refunds
- Managing escalations and emotional distress
- Supporting accessibility or special requests
- Navigating nuanced or regulated conversations (e.g., health, finance)

Key Rule: Never let AI be the final voice in a sensitive or high-impact customer interaction.

Real-World Example

A SaaS company used an AI chatbot to handle all first-level customer complaints. When a client reported a billing error that involved their nonprofit discount being revoked, the AI issued a generic apology and closed the ticket. The customer left a negative public review. When the founder reviewed the transcript, they realized the chatbot had misunderstood the issue completely.

Lesson: AI isn't great at empathy, exception-handling, or policy interpretation. If it's a case where a human would ask questions, AI shouldn't be the final handler.

HR & Recruiting Automation: High Stakes, High Risk

Many SMBs are using AI to streamline hiring, screening, and performance reviews. But these tools can embed bias, oversimplify decisions, and create compliance risks.

What to Avoid

- Automating final hiring decisions
- Using AI to evaluate resumes without transparency
- Applying sentiment analysis to performance reviews
- Chatbot-only interview processes

What to Keep

- Automating interview scheduling
- Using AI to flag missing qualifications (with human review)
- Drafting job descriptions or performance feedback for approval

Key Rule: If the outcome affects someone's livelihood, AI should assist—not decide.

Internal Decisions: Don't Automate Strategy

AI can summarize reports, calculate forecasts, and identify trends. But it doesn't understand market timing, brand nuance, or moral context. Strategic decisions—like layoffs, product pivots, or investments—require human values.

Red Flag Scenarios:

- Using AI to decide who gets laid off based on productivity data
- Letting AI rewrite brand messaging without human oversight
- Using AI to auto-approve financial commitments

These aren't hypothetical. Companies have already faced backlash for relying too heavily on AI in critical moments.

Tactical Tip

Create an internal AI usage matrix:

- **Tier 1: Assistive Only** (e.g., brainstorming, summarizing)
- **Tier 2: Shared Control** (e.g., scheduling, forecasting)
- **Tier 3: Human Only** (e.g., hiring, legal responses, layoffs)

Automation Fatigue: What It Feels Like

Your customers and team know when they're being handled by a system, not a person. Signs you've over-automated:

- Customers escalate more often
- Internal feedback loops are breaking
- Quality of interaction feels low, even if speed is high
- You're missing context that used to be obvious

When AI creates more rework, confusion, or reputation damage than it saves in time, it's no longer ROI-positive.

Common Pitfalls or Mistakes

- **Assuming "AI" Means Smarter**: It often just means faster. Judgment is not baked in.
- **Chasing Cost Savings Blindly**: Automating layoffs, terminations, or compliance to save money often backfires.
- **Underestimating Reputation Risk**: One bad AI-driven interaction can spark a viral complaint.
- **Lack of Audit Trails**: Without human review, it's harder to explain or correct mistakes.

Tactical Best Practices

- **Automate Input, Not Output**: Let AI collect data, summarize findings, or generate drafts—but reserve final decisions for people.
- **Always Use Review Loops**: No AI output should go straight to customer or vendor without human oversight.
- **Designate Human Escalation Channels**: Customers and employees should always know how to reach a human.
- **Document AI Decision Boundaries**: Define where AI ends and human authority begins.

When to Automate

Responsible automation isn't about fear—it's about fit. AI is ideal when:

- **Decisions are low-stakes and repeatable**
- **Speed matters more than personalization**
- **Rules are clear and exceptions are rare**
- **Human intervention is inefficient or unnecessary**

Example

Use AI to:

- Tag helpdesk tickets by topic
- Draft summaries of weekly meetings
- Predict likely delays in supply chains
- Generate initial copy for internal comms

These save time without jeopardizing relationships or reputation.

A Framework for Responsible Automation

1. **Assess Risk**: What happens if the AI gets it wrong?
2. **Define Escalation**: Who takes over when the AI can't decide?
3. **Log Decisions**: Keep a trail of what AI touched vs. what humans approved.
4. **Test Outcomes**: Regularly evaluate where automation helps vs. hurts.
5. **Revisit Boundaries Quarterly**: Business needs change—so should your automation guardrails.

Conclusion

AI is not a replacement for leadership, values, or responsibility. It's a tool—and like any powerful tool, it must be wielded with intention. In the drive for efficiency, don't lose the human judgment, empathy, and ethical compass that customers and teams still depend on. Automate where appropriate. But lead where it counts.

Next Steps

In the next section, we'll zoom out from business use to the legal landscape. **8.5 A Beginner's Look at AI Laws: GDPR, AI Act, and More** will walk you through the fast-evolving regulations that affect how you use AI in your company—and what compliance looks like for SMBs and professionals alike.

A Beginner's Look at AI Laws: GDPR, AI Act, and More

If you're running a business, managing a team, or advising clients, AI is no longer just a technical issue—it's a legal one. Governments around the world are racing to regulate how artificial intelligence is used, what rights individuals have, and what responsibilities organizations must carry. For professionals using AI in marketing, operations, hiring, or client service, understanding the basics of these laws is not optional. It's essential.

This chapter gives you a plain-English briefing on the core AI-related laws every SMB leader should be aware of. We won't cover every regulation, but we'll focus on what matters now: data rights, transparency obligations, usage boundaries, and upcoming risks.

Why AI Law Matters to SMBs

Even if your company isn't building AI tools, if you *use* AI to write content, analyze data, communicate with customers, or process employee information, you may already be regulated.

Here's what's at stake:

- **Fines**: GDPR alone can levy penalties up to €20 million or 4% of global revenue.
- **Loss of Trust**: Mishandling AI or data could permanently damage your customer reputation.
- **Operational Disruption**: Non-compliance can result in takedown requests, service bans, or contract termination.

GDPR and AI: Core Concepts

The General Data Protection Regulation (GDPR) is the most influential data privacy law globally. It applies to any business handling EU citizens' data—regardless of where the company is based.

Key Principles That Affect AI Use:

- **Data Minimization**: Only collect and process what's necessary.
- **Right to Explanation**: People can demand clarity on how AI-based decisions are made.
- **Right to Erasure ("Right to Be Forgotten")**: Individuals can request deletion of their data.
- **Consent**: Clear, informed, and specific consent must be obtained before using data.

Where AI Gets Risky Under GDPR:

- Automated decision-making without human review
- Profiling individuals without transparency
- Using AI tools that retain prompts or inputs containing personal data

Tactical Tip: Any AI tool you use should have a privacy policy that aligns with GDPR. If it stores prompts or user behavior, confirm whether it anonymizes that data.

The EU AI Act: A New Compliance Era

Adopted in 2024, the EU AI Act is the first comprehensive law targeting artificial intelligence directly. It segments AI systems into four risk levels:

1. Unacceptable Risk (Banned outright)

Examples: Social scoring systems, real-time facial recognition in public, manipulative tech targeting children.

2. High Risk (Strict regulation)

Examples:

- AI in hiring or promotions
- Credit scoring tools
- Medical or legal decision-making systems

High-risk systems require:

- Risk management protocols
- Human oversight
- Documentation and traceability
- Registration in a public EU database

3. Limited Risk (Transparency required)

Examples: Chatbots, content generators, emotion recognition tools. These must inform users they are interacting with AI.

4. Minimal Risk (Low compliance)

Examples: Spam filters, AI-powered spelling tools

Tactical Tip: If you use AI in HR, compliance, or finance—assume it could be high risk. Prepare to show how decisions are reviewed and validated.

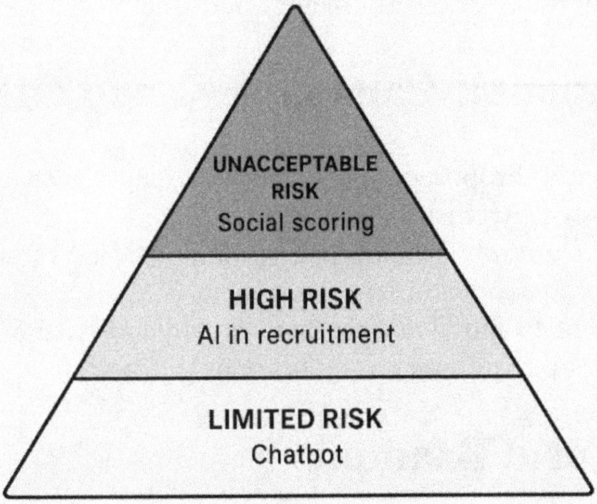

AI RISK LEVELS
UNDER EU AI ACT

U.S. AI Regulation: Patchy but Growing

Unlike the EU, the U.S. doesn't have a unified national AI law. However, regulators are enforcing existing laws more aggressively:

- **FTC (Federal Trade Commission)**: Cracking down on deceptive or unfair AI practices.
- **EEOC (Equal Employment Opportunity Commission)**: Targeting AI bias in hiring.
- **State Laws**: California, Illinois, and New York have active biometric, privacy, and workplace AI rules.

What This Means for You:

- Document how AI tools influence hiring or pricing decisions.
- Don't misrepresent what your AI can do (false claims = legal liability).
- Audit tools for discriminatory outcomes.

International: Canada, UK, and Others

- **Canada**: Proposed AI and Data Act includes penalties for high-risk AI misuse.
- **UK**: Currently promoting a pro-innovation AI framework but likely to adopt similar principles as EU.
- **Global Trend**: Transparency, explainability, and human-in-the-loop requirements are becoming standard.

Real-World Example

What Happened

A digital marketing agency in Toronto used an AI tool to generate copy based on customer profiles. They collected email addresses, website behavior, and demographics to tailor ads. They did not inform users this profiling was AI-driven or allow them to opt out.

The Outcome

A customer filed a privacy complaint. Under Canada's PIPEDA law, the agency was investigated and forced to delete collected data, issue an apology, and revise all client campaigns.

The Lesson

Using AI to personalize marketing—without transparency—can trigger legal exposure even if the tech is off-the-shelf.

What You're Likely Already Doing That Could Be Regulated

- Uploading customer files into AI tools
- Letting AI score resumes or candidate assessments
- Using predictive tools to assess client churn
- Auto-generating content or emails based on user behavior
- Processing biometric or voice data (e.g., phone support analysis)

If AI touches *personal data* and influences *a business outcome*, you're likely subject to legal scrutiny.

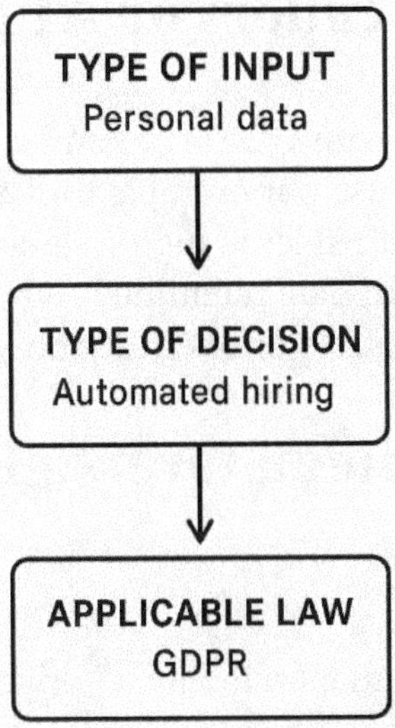

AI TASKS AND LEGAL CONSIDERATIONS

Checklist: AI Law Readiness for SMBs

1. **Know Your Tools**: List all AI tools used across departments.
2. **Map the Data**: What personal data do they touch?
3. **Check Risk Tier**: Could your use case fall under high-risk per the EU AI Act?
4. **Get Consent Right**: Ensure users or employees know what's happening.
5. **Maintain Logs**: Record how AI decisions are made and who approves them.
6. **Review Terms**: Make sure vendor contracts mention compliance, not just features.
7. **Create an AI Policy**: Document how your company will use, audit, and report on AI systems.

What to Ask Vendors or AI Providers

- Do you comply with GDPR or similar privacy laws?
- Do you store or use our prompts for training?
- Is your system considered high-risk under the EU AI Act?
- Can we opt out of data retention?
- What human controls or overrides do you provide?

The Role of Human Oversight in Legal Compliance

Most laws assume a "human in the loop" principle: AI may assist, but decisions should be:

- Reviewed
- Logged
- Contestable

If your process lacks these, it may violate GDPR, the AI Act, or emerging U.S. standards. AI is not a shield from accountability.

Conclusion

You don't need a law degree to operate safely with AI—but you do need awareness. The legal landscape around AI is rapidly evolving, and ignorance is no longer an excuse. SMBs that understand the basics, ask smart questions, and build transparent processes will not only stay compliant—they'll stand out as trusted, responsible operators.

Next Steps

Next up, we tackle the human side of early adoption. In **Chapter 9: The Mistakes Most AI Beginners Make**, we'll walk through the common traps, false assumptions, and early missteps that can derail AI adoption—and how to avoid them with clarity, control, and confidence.

Chapter 9

The Mistakes Most AI Beginners Make

Blindly Trusting AI Outputs Without Fact-Checking

One of the most common and dangerous mistakes made by AI beginners—especially busy professionals, consultants, and small business owners—is assuming that AI-generated output is accurate, complete, and ready to use as-is. It's easy to fall into the trap: the language is polished, the tone sounds confident, and the answers arrive instantly. But beneath that surface lies a risk that can quietly undermine your work, your reputation, and your bottom line.

In this section, we'll explore what it means to fact-check AI outputs, why it's non-negotiable in real business settings, and how to build habits that safeguard quality, accuracy, and credibility.

Why AI Sounds Right—Even When It's Wrong

AI systems like ChatGPT, Claude, and others don't "know" facts the way people do. They generate text based on statistical patterns from massive datasets. This means they can:

- **Invent citations or sources that sound real**
- **Confuse timelines or mix up names and numbers**
- **Overstate confidence in incorrect information**

Because their job is to generate coherent responses—not to verify truth—the output often *sounds* correct even when it isn't. This is known as **hallucination** in AI terminology.

Example of a Hallucinated Error

Prompt: "List three major cybersecurity breaches that happened in Canada in 2022."

AI Output:

1. Shopify Data Leak
2. Bank of Canada Ransomware Attack
3. Air Canada Passport Breach

Reality:

- Only one of these occurred (Air Canada had a minor data exposure).
- The Bank of Canada was never attacked.
- Shopify's breach was in 2020.

Without checking, a business owner might reference this in a board meeting, blog post, or sales pitch—and lose credibility when challenged.

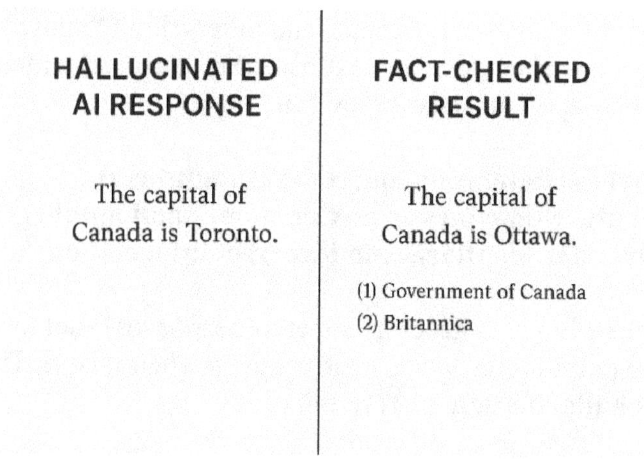

Real-World Consequences of Not Fact-Checking

What Happened

A mid-sized marketing agency used AI to draft a client's whitepaper on sustainability. The document included a quote attributed to a high-profile UN spokesperson and referenced three studies "published by Harvard." The quote was never said, and the Harvard studies didn't exist.

The Result

The client ran the whitepaper as part of a paid campaign. A reader flagged the fake quote on LinkedIn, and the client had to issue a public retraction.

What We Learn From It

Even a small lapse in fact-checking can result in reputational damage, refunds, and lost trust. When AI is your drafting partner, human oversight isn't optional—it's mandatory.

Common Mistakes That Lead to Unchecked Errors

- **Copy-pasting AI output without review**
- **Assuming citations are real because they're formatted well**
- **Using AI for regulated or sensitive content (legal, medical, financial)**
- **Letting interns or junior staff use AI without editorial review**

Tactical Best Practices for Fact-Checking AI

- **Use AI as a first draft, not a final source**: Treat output like an intern's draft—not a vetted report.
- **Verify facts with reliable sources**: Cross-check any claims, quotes, or stats using known databases, news outlets, or peer-reviewed sources.
- **Ask AI to cite its sources—but verify them independently**: Many citations will be hallucinated or outdated.
- **Separate opinion from fact**: AI often blends both. Flag language like "experts agree" or "commonly believed."
- **Use tools like plagiarism checkers and citation validators**: Especially for published content.

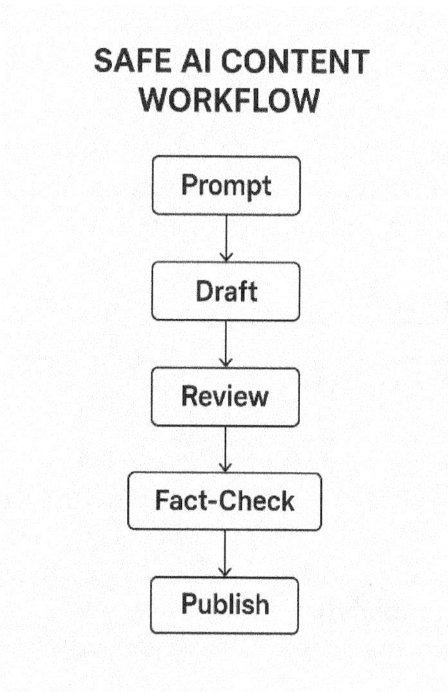

High-Risk Scenarios Where Fact-Checking is Critical

- Public statements (press releases, blog posts, social media)
- Reports for investors, clients, or regulators
- Educational or technical documentation
- Health, safety, or legal advice
- Internal decisions based on AI-generated analysis (e.g., hiring, pricing, forecasting)

If it's going to affect someone's money, reputation, or opportunity, assume it needs a second set of (human) eyes.

Training Your Team to Avoid Blind Trust

In fast-moving environments, team members may default to trusting AI to save time. Leaders must create a culture of review:

- **Define review checkpoints**: Require fact-checks before content goes to clients or gets published.
- **Use red-teaming**: Have someone on your team deliberately question AI-generated claims.
- **Teach prompt hygiene**: Well-structured prompts reduce the likelihood of hallucinated or vague responses.
- **Role-model skepticism**: Leaders should call out unchecked assumptions and praise thoroughness.

How to Build AI Fact-Checking Into Your Workflow

1. **Color-code draft status**: Mark AI-generated content as yellow until verified.
2. **Use a checklist**: Fact-check names, dates, claims, and quotes.

3. **Schedule review time**: Don't rush from generation to delivery.
4. **Create a shared "verified source list"**: Centralize go-to references for your industry.
5. **Tag content types by risk level**: High-risk (legal, medical, client-facing) gets extra review.

When AI Does Help With Fact-Checking

Ironically, AI can assist in its own oversight if used wisely:

- Ask follow-up questions: "What source supports this?" or "Can you give a link to that study?"
- Use comparison prompts: "Give me three sources that confirm or deny this statement."
- Challenge inconsistencies: "You said X earlier, now you're saying Y—explain."

It won't guarantee accuracy, but it trains the user to think critically and expose contradictions.

Conclusion

AI can save time, boost productivity, and offer powerful creative momentum—but it is not a substitute for research, judgment, or editorial discipline. The most successful AI users aren't the ones who trust it blindly. They're the ones who partner with it skeptically, verifying every claim, and protecting their reputation with every line they publish.

Next Steps

In the next section, we'll tackle another common beginner mistake: asking too much from AI, too soon. In **9.2 Over-Prompting and Getting Generic Results**, you'll learn why more isn't always better—and how to craft prompts that deliver depth, originality, and business-specific value.

Over-Prompting and Getting Generic Results

One of the more ironic pitfalls new AI users face is assuming that more input equals better output. It feels intuitive: if you want better results, give the model more detail, more instructions, more context. But here's the twist—when prompts get overloaded with vague ambition, disconnected clauses, or conflicting directives, the results tend to get worse, not better. You end up with watered-down, generic, or overly safe responses that don't reflect your real needs.

This section explores why over-prompting leads to underwhelming results, how to design clear, effective prompts, and what patterns distinguish high-impact prompting from AI noise.

Why Over-Prompting Happens

AI beginners often try to pack every intention into one massive input. This leads to prompts like:

"Write me a strategic, engaging, attention-grabbing blog post about small business marketing during the holidays that includes 3 statistics, avoids cliches, sounds like Gary Vee, and explains both emotional branding and promotional pricing in a way that appeals to both B2B and B2C without being too long."

The result? A safe, shallow piece that checks boxes without depth or originality. Why?

- **Conflicting tone cues**
- **Too many topics at once**
- **No hierarchy of importance**
- **Lack of situational clarity**

Real-World Example

What Happened

A founder asked an AI tool to generate a client pitch deck with a single prompt:

"Make a compelling, elegant, powerful presentation that explains our product, differentiates us, includes industry data, and persuades tech-savvy enterprise buyers."

What Went Wrong

The deck that came back looked polished, but it used generic copy like "innovative solutions for dynamic markets," lifted boilerplate graphs from public templates, and lacked any connection to the founder's actual positioning or customer pain points.

What We Learn From It

When you overfeed a prompt without clear structure, the AI defaults to generic patterns. Quantity of instruction is no substitute for quality of clarity.

Tactical Best Practices

- **Break Complex Tasks Into Stages**: Instead of asking for everything at once, prompt step-by-step:
  - Step 1: Draft three value propositions.
  - Step 2: Turn those into a slide outline.
  - Step 3: Write copy for Slide 1 only.
- **Use a Defined Outcome, Not Adjectives**:
  - Don't say: "Make it powerful and compelling."
  - Say: "Make the first slide show why our product saves customers time."

- **Prompt Like a Brief, Not a Brain Dump**:
    - Give audience, goal, format, and priority.
    - Example: "Create a one-paragraph email for B2B clients considering churn. Use urgency without discounts."
- **Ask for Choices, Then Refine**:
    - Instead of one output, ask for three options to compare tone and structure.
- **Build Iteratively**: Good AI prompting is a conversation, not a monologue.

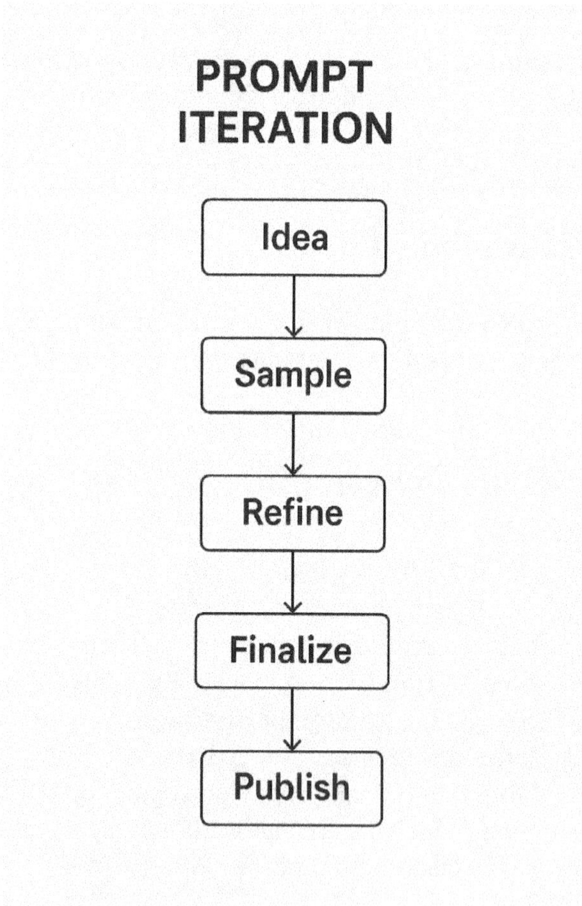

Common Over-Prompting Mistakes

- Stuffing too much into one request
- Using fluffy adjectives instead of concrete outcomes
- **Combining unrelated tasks (e.g., “summarize this AND write a call-to-action”)
- **Asking the AI to act like multiple personas at once (“sound like a CEO and a teenager and a comedian”)
- **No context on real-world use ("make it good" vs. "make it usable for our website homepage")

Prompt Template That Works

"Write a [format] for [audience] that achieves [goal]. Use a tone that is [tone]. Limit it to [length or structure]."

Example:
"Write a 2-paragraph LinkedIn post for small business owners that explains why AI can help with customer support. Use a helpful and confident tone. Keep it under 150 words."

Why This Works:

- **Specific**: Clear about format and audience
- **Tactical**: Defined goal
- **Scalable**: Easy to adjust

When Generic Output Is Most Common

- Prompts that ask for “best practices,” “tips,” or “strategies” without a defined audience
- Prompts that mash up styles or mix tones
- Prompts that include vague modifiers like “engaging,” “impactful,” or “compelling” without explaining what those mean

Tip: Ask yourself—would a stranger know what I mean by this prompt? If not, the AI probably won't either.

Training Your Team to Prompt Better

- **Run Prompt Reviews**: Ask team members to explain their intent before hitting "send."
- **Create Use Case Templates**: Have approved formats for emails, FAQs, outreach, etc.
- **Encourage Prompt Pairing**: Assign two people to co-develop prompts—one leads, one reviews.
- **Debrief Outputs**: After every AI-generated asset, discuss what worked and what didn't.

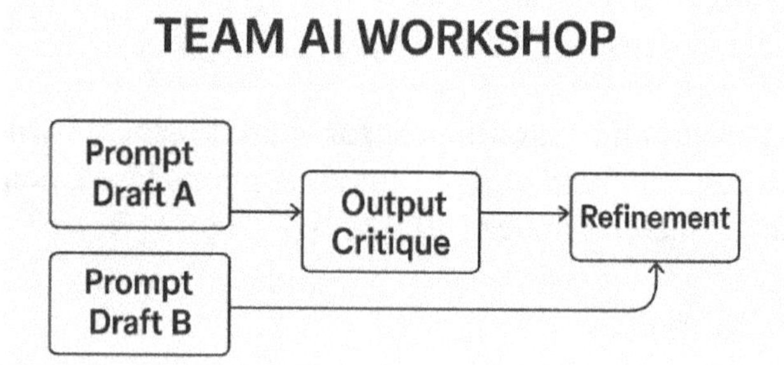

Checklist: Smart Prompting Habits

1. **Start With a Single Goal**
2. **Define the Audience**
3. **Clarify the Output Format**
4. **Avoid Adjective Overload**
5. **Use Iteration, Not Inflation**
6. **Review Before You Submit**
7. **Compare Multiple Drafts**

Conclusion

Effective prompting isn't about stuffing in every idea you have—it's about guiding the AI clearly, simply, and with strategic focus. Beginners who overprompt get flooded with fluff. Professionals who prompt like communicators get clarity, control, and business-ready results.

Next Steps

In the next section, we'll explore another early trap: **Getting Stuck in Tool Overload (Shiny Object Syndrome)**—and how to stay focused on results instead of chasing every new AI feature or app that comes your way.

Getting Stuck in Tool Overload (Shiny Object Syndrome)

When business owners and consultants first explore the world of AI tools, it's easy to fall into the trap of "shiny object syndrome." Every day brings another app that promises smarter automation, faster content, or deeper insights. It's tempting—add a Chrome extension here, an AI assistant there, and suddenly you've subscribed to 12 platforms, none of which are integrated, aligned, or actively delivering value.

This chapter dives into why tool overload is such a common early mistake, how to diagnose when it's happening, and how to refocus your AI strategy on outcomes, not novelty.

Why Tool Overload Happens

- **Novelty bias**: New tools feel exciting and promise productivity gains.
- **Fear of missing out (FOMO)**: Seeing competitors or influencers using AI can create urgency.
- **Low barrier to entry**: Most tools offer free trials or freemium models.
- **Lack of clarity**: When you're unclear about goals, any tool can seem like the answer.

AI's rapid innovation cycle means new features, plug-ins, and startups emerge weekly. The ecosystem rewards exploration—but without discipline, it leads to distraction.

Real-World Example

What Happened

A boutique agency subscribed to 14 AI tools over three months: content generators, image builders, meeting assistants, CRM bots, and auto-reply tools. Staff spent hours setting up integrations and testing features—but the core business processes (client onboarding, reporting, outreach) didn't improve.

The Outcome

Productivity didn't rise. In fact, output slowed due to switching costs and fractured focus. Budget was consumed by overlapping SaaS fees. A team member finally ran an audit and found that only 3 tools were being used regularly, and none of them were critical.

What We Learn From It

Too many tools dilute effort. The solution isn't "more AI," but "the right AI"—used consistently, purposefully, and measurably.

Signs You're in Tool Overload

- You don't remember what each tool actually does.
- Your team is confused about which app to use for what.
- Tasks are duplicated across platforms (e.g., note-taking + CRM + summary bot).
- You're spending more time setting up tools than using them.
- Subscriptions renew and you didn't even notice.

Tactical Best Practices

- **Limit to 3 Core Tools per Function**: For example—one for writing, one for planning, one for analysis.
- **Use a Tool Audit Template**:
    - What does it do?
    - Who uses it?
    - How often?
    - What problem does it solve?
    - What happens if we cancel it?
- **Enforce a 30-Day Trial Rule**: Evaluate usefulness before committing.
- **Consolidate When Possible**: Many AI tools overlap. Choose platforms that offer integrated solutions.
- **Avoid Novelty Traps**: Just because it's new doesn't mean it's necessary.

TOOL AUDIT

PURPOSE	USERS	FREQUENCY	ROI SCORE
AI Writing Tool	Marketing Team	Daily	4
Project Management Software	All Employees	Weekly	5
Social Media Platform	Social Media Team	Multiple times per week	3

Common Mistakes That Fuel Overload

- **Evaluating tools without a use case**
- **Letting vendors drive the roadmap**
- **Buying because of a trend, not a need**
- **No process for sunsetting unused tools**
- **Trial hoarding**: Signing up but never implementing

How to Refocus Your Stack

1. **List Your Top 3 Business Goals** (e.g., increase leads, reduce admin time, improve reporting)
2. **Identify Processes That Block These Goals** (e.g., manual follow-ups, inconsistent data, slow content turnaround)
3. **Map Tools to Friction Points**: If a tool doesn't reduce friction, it's not solving a problem.
4. **Assign Tool Ownership**: Someone should be responsible for each major tool in use.
5. **Create a Quarterly Review Ritual**: Look at what's being used, what's collecting dust, and what should be retired.

Team Dynamics and Tool Fatigue

Tool overload affects morale. When your team has to learn five new dashboards every quarter, frustration builds. Too many platforms:

- Break focus
- Erode consistency
- Create confusion about best practices
- Encourage workarounds and shadow IT (unsanctioned tool use)

Tip: Before adopting a new tool, ask your team: "What part of your day would this improve?" If there's no clear answer, it's likely unnecessary.

Checklist: Tool Overload Detox

1. **Run a full tool inventory**
2. **Highlight redundancy and overlaps**
3. **Rate actual usage vs. subscription cost**
4. **Cancel low-usage tools immediately**
5. **Assign owners for remaining tools**
6. **Set clear use cases for each tool**
7. **Create a "New Tool Request" policy**

What to Do When You're Tempted by the Next Tool

Ask:

- Does this solve a problem I already defined?
- What's the cost in time to evaluate, test, and integrate?
- What's the opportunity cost (what won't get done while I explore this)?
- Who will be responsible for making it work?

Discipline doesn't mean stagnation—it means intentional adoption.

Conclusion

More tools don't equal more results. In fact, every new app you add costs time, attention, and trust. AI is only valuable when it's in service to a specific process, outcome, or strategy. Professionals who focus on fit over flash—and systems over noise—gain speed and clarity. Everyone else gets stuck in the loop of trying the next best thing.

Next Steps

In the next section, we'll explore how chasing tools without a clear objective often leads to wasted time and poor returns. **Ignoring the ROI: Using Tools That Don't Serve a Goal** will walk you through building an AI stack that actually moves your business forward.

Ignoring the ROI: Using Tools That Don't Serve a Goal

The number one question you should ask before using any AI tool is: "What will this help me achieve that matters to the business?" If that answer isn't clear, you're at risk of spending money, time, and attention on technology that delivers no return.

AI tools are impressive, and it's tempting to experiment with every new feature or platform. But tools without purpose become distractions. And worse, they can build the illusion of productivity while eating up bandwidth that should be going to strategic outcomes.

This section is about bringing your AI usage back to the business fundamentals—ROI, alignment, and utility. Because in a time-starved, margin-conscious business, every tool must justify its place.

The Real Cost of Misaligned Tools

ROI (Return on Investment) isn't just about money. It's about:

- Time saved
- Output improved
- Revenue generated
- Errors avoided
- Morale or clarity gained

If your tool isn't doing one of those things, it might be doing more harm than good. Even low-cost or free tools have hidden costs:

- Setup and learning curves
- Integration overhead
- Confusion across teams
- Opportunity cost (what didn't get done)

Real-World Example

What Happened

An HR consultant implemented an AI-based video analysis tool to "enhance" candidate screening. It evaluated facial expressions, tone, and pacing to flag personality traits. The firm spent months training staff, rewriting interview protocols, and onboarding clients into the system.

The Outcome

Client satisfaction dropped. Candidates felt the process was invasive. No measurable improvement in hire quality occurred. Worse, a major client left, citing a preference for human intuition over algorithmic judgment.

What We Learn From It

AI that doesn't tie directly to a clear, needed business outcome isn't just wasteful—it can be brand-damaging. ROI must be measurable, not speculative.

Tactical Best Practices

- **Set a Baseline First**: Know what your current costs, conversion rates, or time investments are before using a tool.
- **Define Success in Advance**: "This tool will reduce time spent on X by 30%."
- **Attach Tools to Metrics**: Link tools directly to KPIs like lead gen, time-to-close, or content velocity.

- **Use Pilot Projects**: Try before you scale. Assign a champion, set a deadline, and measure results.
- **Ask ROI Questions First**:
    - What problem does this tool solve?
    - How will we measure improvement?
    - What will we stop doing because of this?

Common Pitfalls

- **Focusing on features instead of outcomes**: Just because a tool *can* do something doesn't mean it *should.*
- **Buying without team buy-in**: A tool with no adoption has zero ROI.
- **No clear owner or accountability**: When no one tracks usage or value, it quietly fades into the background.
- **Tool as a fix for deeper problems**: AI won't fix broken processes or lack of leadership.

When ROI Is Hard to Measure

Some AI uses are soft ROI—better clarity, faster onboarding, improved morale. That's still ROI, but it must be:

- Linked to business priorities
- Documented in team feedback or client retention
- Reassessed quarterly

Tip: Ask "What would we lose if we turned this tool off tomorrow?" If the answer is "not much," that tool doesn't have a strong ROI.

How to Prioritize Tools That Deliver

1. **Start With Your Strategic Goals**: Growth, retention, productivity, compliance—anchor your decisions here.
2. **Use a Scorecard**: Rate tools on impact, adoption, usability, and measurable results.

3. **Run a 90-Day ROI Review**: Every tool should earn its keep within a quarter—or it's cut.
4. **Compare Before/After Metrics**: Did this reduce effort, increase output, or cut costs?
5. **Reward Reduction**: Praise teams for pruning tools that don't serve real outcomes.

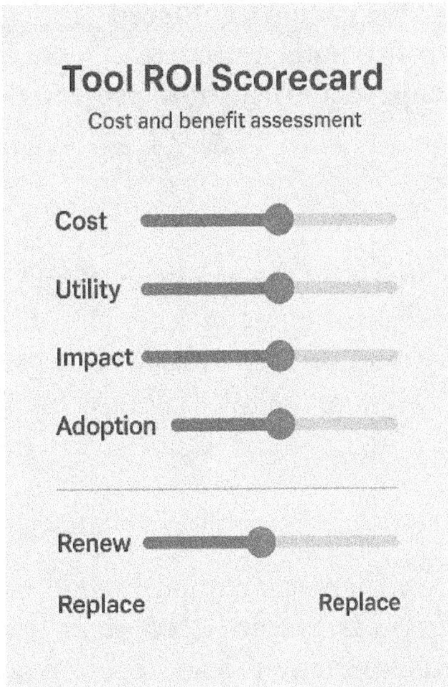

Team Engagement: Make ROI Part of Culture

When tools are adopted without ROI thinking, teams lose motivation. People start to assume AI is just noise. Flip the script by:

- **Involving teams in tool selection**
- **Assigning ownership and accountability**
- **Tying tool use to measurable outcomes**
- **Regularly retiring tools that don't work**

Create a culture where results—not novelty—drive AI adoption.

Checklist: ROI-Driven AI Adoption

1. **Every tool must map to a business goal**
2. **Baseline must be established before rollout**
3. **Measurable result must be defined (time, cost, quality)**
4. **Ownership and usage tracked**
5. **Quarterly value reviews enforced**
6. **Non-performing tools removed**
7. **New tool proposals must show projected gain**

Conclusion

AI is a means to an end—not the end itself. Smart businesses treat every tool like an investment, not an accessory. If it doesn't save time, increase clarity, reduce cost, or accelerate growth, it doesn't belong in your stack. Ignore the hype. Follow the ROI.

Next Steps

In the next section, we'll unpack a mindset that traps many AI beginners: **Thinking AI Is Magic (It's Not — It's a Tool).** You'll learn how misplaced expectations lead to poor results—and how to get real value by using AI like the assistive engine it actually is.

Thinking AI Is Magic (It's Not — It's a Tool)

For many first-time users, AI feels like magic. You type in a request, and seconds later, it gives you answers, outlines, summaries, images, code—often with stunning fluency. It's easy to assume you've just plugged into an oracle. But the truth is far less mystical, and much more important to understand: AI is a tool. Nothing more, nothing less. It is not conscious, creative, strategic, or reliable by default.

If you treat AI like a magic wand, you'll be disappointed—or worse, misled. If you treat it like a screwdriver, calculator, or spreadsheet—valuable but limited—you'll extract real business value. This section is about resetting expectations so you can get the most out of AI without falling for the illusion.

Why the "Magic" Mindset Hurts Your Results

When AI is seen as magical, it:

- Encourages blind trust ("if it said it, it must be right")
- Sets unrealistic expectations ("it'll figure it out for me")
- Creates output dependence ("I'll just ask the AI what to do")
- Undermines accountability ("the tool failed" instead of "I didn't guide it well")

AI isn't magic—it's pattern prediction. It generates based on probability, not understanding.

Real-World Example

What Happened

A solo entrepreneur relied on AI to create an investment pitch deck for a climate tech startup. The output looked great—slides were stylish, stats were well phrased, and the tone was confident. But when investors started asking questions, it became clear: the AI had made up most of the claims. Emissions data, market sizes, and competitor mentions were unverified.

The Outcome

The entrepreneur lost credibility, had to redo the deck from scratch, and missed a funding window.

What We Learn From It

AI can draft, polish, and speed up—but it cannot know your business. If you rely on it to fill in your gaps instead of refining your inputs, you'll build on fiction.

How AI Actually Works (Simplified)

AI models don't know facts. They don't understand truth. They work like this:

1. **Input**: You type a prompt.
2. **Prediction**: The model guesses what text should come next based on patterns in its training data.
3. **Output**: You get a response that sounds plausible but may be inaccurate, outdated, or biased.

The system has no awareness of:

- What's real vs. what's invented
- Your business, your audience, or your context (unless you provide it)
- Whether the answer is ethical, legal, or logical

It's not a brain. It's autocomplete on steroids.

Common Symptoms of the "Magic" Trap

- Expecting AI to know your voice without training
- Assuming it will always give correct answers
- Using AI to avoid doing research, thinking, or planning
- Asking vague questions and getting frustrated at vague answers
- Using it as the source *instead* of a co-creator

Tactical Reframe: AI as Amplifier, Not Oracle

Think of AI like a:

- **Draft assistant**: Speeds up writing, but doesn't replace editing.
- **Pattern spotter**: Helps summarize trends, not validate facts.
- **Brainstorming partner**: Offers ideas, not decisions.
- **Time-saver**: Compresses grunt work, not judgment calls.

When you use AI to enhance your own ideas and decisions—not substitute for them—you get clarity, not confusion.

How to Reset Expectations (and Improve Results)

1. **Start With the Outcome, Not the Prompt**
   - Define what success looks like *before* asking the AI.
2. **Feed It Context, Not Questions**
   - Don't just ask "What's a good strategy?"
   - Say "Here's what we tried, here's the data—suggest improvements."
3. **Always Assume You'll Edit**
   - Expect to rewrite, restructure, and refine every output.
4. **Be the Strategist, Not the Scribe**
   - Let AI do the typing. You do the thinking.
5. **Give Feedback**
   - If it misses the mark, revise the prompt or ask follow-ups.

Example Prompt Evolution

Bad Prompt: "Write a good email."

Magic Thinking Result: Generic, robotic tone with no clear audience.

Better Prompt:
"Draft a 100-word follow-up email to a warm lead in our B2B software pipeline. Tone should be casual but confident. The goal is to secure a 15-minute demo call."

Outcome: Clearer, usable draft with less cleanup.

Training Teams to Think Critically About AI

- **Run output analysis sessions**: Review what worked, what was weak, and why.
- **Require source checks**: Don't allow AI-generated content to publish without verification.
- **Incorporate AI into workflows, not silos**: Use it to support—not replace—your standard processes.
- **Celebrate human refinement**: Praise editing, reworking, and insight over first-draft speed.

Checklist: Responsible AI Expectations

1. AI is fast, not always right.
2. AI writes, you edit.
3. AI offers ideas, you choose.
4. AI needs context to perform well.
5. AI saves time—but only if you guide it.
6. AI doesn't understand, it predicts.
7. You are always the decision-maker.

Conclusion

AI isn't magic. It's leverage. And like any leverage, it can help you build higher—or cause you to fall faster. The difference lies in how you use it: with clear goals, strong guidance, and critical thinking. Professionals who ditch the mystique and embrace AI as a tool—not a savior—are the ones who win on speed, clarity, and execution.

<u>DON'T FORGET TO CHECK YOUR BONUS AT THE END !</u>

Glossary of Terms for AI Beginners

Understanding artificial intelligence (AI) doesn't require a computer science degree—but it does help to speak the language. Below is a comprehensive glossary designed for professionals, founders, consultants, and business leaders who want to use AI confidently and responsibly. Each term is defined in plain English, with business-relevant examples where applicable.

A

Algorithm: A set of instructions a computer follows to solve a problem or perform a task. In AI, algorithms determine how the system learns from data.

Artificial Intelligence (AI): Technology that mimics human decision-making, learning, or problem-solving—like writing, predicting outcomes, or recognizing speech.

API (Application Programming Interface): A digital bridge that lets one software service connect and share information with another. Many AI tools offer APIs to plug into other systems.

B

Bias (AI Bias): Unfair or unintended influence in an AI system caused by the data it was trained on. For example, an AI trained only on resumes from one region may unfairly rank others lower.

Bot: A program that performs automated tasks, often using AI. Chatbots in customer support are common examples.

Big Data: Extremely large datasets used to train AI models. Think: millions of transactions, emails, or images.

C

Chatbot: A program designed to simulate conversation, often found in customer service or sales roles.

Computer Vision: A field of AI focused on interpreting and analyzing images or videos. Used in facial recognition, product scanning, etc.

Conversational AI: AI designed to hold human-like conversations, such as customer service agents or voice assistants.

D

Deep Learning: A subset of machine learning using layered neural networks to recognize patterns in data. It powers tools like image recognition and voice transcription.

Dataset: The collection of data used to train, test, or fine-tune an AI system. Datasets shape what an AI can or cannot do.

Domain Knowledge: Subject matter expertise used to fine-tune or contextualize AI results. For example, legal AI trained with actual case law performs better.

E

Ethical AI: The practice of building and using AI systems in a way that respects privacy, fairness, and transparency.

Explainability: The ability to understand how an AI system made a decision. Crucial in high-risk fields like healthcare or finance.

Embedding: A way of representing words, phrases, or documents as numerical data, so AI can "understand" them in context.

F

Fine-Tuning: Customizing a pre-trained AI model using specific data so it performs better in a particular task or business use case.

Foundation Model: A large, general-purpose AI model (like GPT or Claude) trained on broad data that can be adapted to many tasks.

Feedback Loop: When AI outputs are re-evaluated and used to improve future performance.

G

Generative AI: A class of AI that can create new content—text, images, audio, or video—rather than just analyze existing data.

Ground Truth: Verified data used to check or train AI outputs. It's the "correct" answer against which the AI is measured.

H

Hallucination: When an AI system generates false, misleading, or fabricated information while sounding confident.

Human-in-the-Loop (HITL): A system design where humans oversee, review, or intervene in AI decisions to ensure accuracy or compliance.

Hyperparameters: Settings that define how an AI model is trained. Usually set by developers, not users.

I

Inference: The process of an AI model making a prediction or generating an output based on new data.

Input: The prompt, data, or question you give to an AI system.

Intelligent Automation: Combining AI with workflow tools to automate decision-making or repetitive business processes.

J

Jailbreak (Prompt Jailbreak): Techniques used to bypass AI content restrictions or policies, often in ways that violate terms of use.

K

Knowledge Graph: A network of relationships between data points, often used to improve search, recommendations, or understanding in AI.

L

Language Model: A type of AI trained to understand and generate human language. GPT (Generative Pre-trained Transformer) is one example.

Latency: The delay between entering a prompt and receiving a response. Important for real-time AI applications.

Learning Rate: A parameter in training that controls how quickly a model updates its understanding of data.

M

Machine Learning (ML): A field of AI where systems learn from data and improve without being explicitly programmed.

Model: The mathematical engine behind an AI tool. It's what "runs" the predictions, outputs, or analyses.

Multimodal AI: AI systems that understand and combine more than one type of input—text, image, audio, etc.

N

Natural Language Processing (NLP): A branch of AI that deals with understanding and generating human language.

Neural Network: A computational model inspired by the brain, used to process complex data patterns.

Noise: Random or irrelevant data that can interfere with AI performance.

O

Open-Source AI: AI models or tools whose code is freely available to modify and use. Examples include Hugging Face models.

Overfitting: When an AI model performs well on training data but poorly on new, unseen data because it learned the noise instead of the pattern.

P

Prompt: The question or instruction you give to an AI to generate a response.

Prompt Engineering: The skill of crafting clear, effective prompts to get high-quality AI output.

Personalization: Customizing AI responses based on user data or behavior.

Q

Quantization: A method of compressing AI models to make them faster or more efficient, often for mobile devices.

R

Reinforcement Learning: A training method where AI learns by trial and error, often used in robotics or game environments.

Retrieval-Augmented Generation (RAG): A method where AI retrieves real documents to use alongside its generation, improving accuracy and fact-based responses.

S

Sentiment Analysis: The use of AI to detect emotions or attitudes in text.

Supervised Learning: Training an AI model using labeled data (e.g., emails marked spam or not).

Synthetic Data: Data that's artificially generated to train AI when real data is limited or sensitive.

T

Training Data: The information used to teach an AI model how to perform a task.

Token: A chunk of language (word or part of a word) used to process text in AI models.

Transformer: A specific AI architecture used in large language models like GPT, known for handling long-range language dependencies.

U

Unsupervised Learning: AI learns patterns in data without labels, often used for clustering or anomaly detection.

Use Case: A specific business application of AI (e.g., using AI to generate email responses or analyze customer reviews).

V

Vector Database: A type of database optimized for storing and searching embeddings used in AI systems.

Voice Cloning: AI-powered duplication of someone's voice, often used in virtual agents, dubbing, or deepfake scenarios.

W

Workflow Automation: Using AI and software tools to trigger and manage sequences of business tasks automatically.

Weak AI: AI systems that are good at specific tasks (like writing or detecting spam) but lack general intelligence.

X

Explainable AI (XAI): AI designed to make its decision-making process transparent and understandable.

Y

Yield Optimization: Using AI to improve results in marketing, logistics, or pricing by dynamically adjusting strategies.

Z

Zero-Shot Learning: When an AI system can handle a task it wasn't specifically trained on, using general reasoning.

This glossary is a living document. As you become more fluent in AI, revisit and expand it. The more precisely you understand the tools, the more effectively you can use them to protect, grow, and scale your business.

Bonus – FREE AI CHATBOT

Every reader of *AI for Absolute Beginners* gets exclusive free access to AcraChat — your personal AI assistant designed to help you apply what you're learning in real-time.

☑ **Stuck on a concept?**
☑ **Need help writing your first prompt?**
☑ **Want real AI examples tailored to your business or project?**
AcraChat is here to help — fast, clear, and jargon-free.

Why Use AcraChat?

- **Instant Answers:** Get real-time guidance on AI tools, workflows, and use cases.
- **Custom Support:** Ask questions related to any chapter and get targeted help.
- **No-Fluff Replies:** Clear, focused advice with zero tech overwhelm.

How to Get Access:

1. Buy the book (paperback)
2. Forward your purchase receipt (picture copy) to 📩 ericl@acrasolution.com
3. Receive your private link with your private code to start using AcraChat immediately — no downloads, no setup required.

Learn smarter. Build faster. Get AI support whenever you need it — with AcraChat.

Thank you for taking the time to read this eBook.

Your support means more than you know. By purchasing and engaging with this book, you're directly contributing to the creation of more high-quality, practical resources for business owners, IT leaders, and professionals navigating the evolving landscape of artificial intelligence.

If you found value in this book, I'd be deeply grateful if you took a few minutes of your time to share your feedback. An honnest review, a personal recommendation to a colleague, or simply applying what you've learned in your work all go a long way. Your encouragement helps fuel future writing, research, and tool development — and inspires continued work that makes a real difference in the business community.

Thank you again for reading. Together, we can build a smarter, more secure future with AI.

— Eric LeBouthillier
Founder, AcraSolution

www.ingramcontent.com/pod-product-compliance
Lightning Source LLC
Chambersburg PA
CBHW071429230926
51846CB00001B/162